THE ALL-NEW OFFICIAL

Arsenal

MISCELLANY

THE ALL-NEW OFFICIAL

Arsenal

MISCELLANY

CHAS NEWKEY-BURDEN

hamlyn

ACKNOWLEDGEMENTS

With grateful thanks to Shehryar Shafiq, Tony Churchill, Samir Singh Nathoo, Mark Payne, Trevor Davies, Charles Hallam, Iain Cook, Andy Exley, Joe Cohen, Tom Watt, Yosef Herzog, Suzi Weizmann, Tony Willis, Andrew Shields, Eleanor Levy, Henry Winter, James and Edward Freedman, Matthew Collin, Matt Ford, Benjamin Netanyahu, Julie Burchill, Martin Corteel, Chris Bevan, Laura Sandell, Anna Southgate, Fiona Robertson, Tokiko Morishima and David Manson. Thanks also to my family: Chris, George, Ieva, Tristan, Penelope, Rose, May and Verity.

Extract from *We All Live in a Perry Groves World* by Perry Groves published by John Blake Publishing. Used by permission of John Blake Publishing.

Executive Editor **Trevor Davies**
Project Editor **Fiona Robertson**
Design Manager **Tokiko Morishima**
Design **'OME DESIGN**
Senior Production Controller **Martin Croshaw**

An Hachette Livre UK Company

First published in Great Britain in 2007
by Hamlyn, a division of Octopus
Publishing Group Ltd
2–4 Heron Quays, London E14 4JP
www.octopusbooks.co.uk

Copyright © Octopus Publishing Group
Ltd 2007

ISBN-13: 978-0-600-61662-7
ISBN-10: 0-600-61662-7

A CIP catalogue record for this book is
available from the British Library

Printed and bound in Slovenia

10 9 8 7 6 5 4 3 2 1

All statistics correct to the end of the 2006/07
season. While the publishers have made every
effort to trace copyright holders of all material
supplied for use in this book, we would like to
apologize for any errors or omissions.

 Arsenal is a registered trademark of
Arsenal Football Club Plc © 2007

FOREWORD

When I first began working for Arsenal in 1946, I couldn't have foreseen the role that the Club would play in my life. Now, over 60 years on, I am delighted to have played a part in one of the most significant events in the illustrious history of this great Club. The move to Emirates Stadium in 2006 marked the beginning of a new chapter in Arsenal's history, and I had the privilege to work on the project right from its conception. The magnificent stadium that we have today is a testament to the great courage, drive and foresight of the Club. The first season at Emirates Stadium, full of scintillating football and world-class stars, has given me an immense amount of enjoyment and confidence in the Club's future.

During my time at Highbury, I have been lucky enough to witness some of the greatest footballers of all time ply their trade on the Highbury turf. From Liam Brady to Thierry Henry, Frank McLintock to Tony Adams, David Rocastle to Dennis Bergkamp, the list of extraordinary players who have pulled on the red and white of Arsenal is endless. With the current crop of great young players brought to the Club by Arsène Wenger, I look forward to seeing even more stars entertaining the crowds at Emirates Stadium over the coming years.

When I think back to the beginning of my Arsenal career, I feel privileged to have seen, and been a small part of, so much. As a youngster I was told, 'Find a job that you really love doing and you will never have to work another day in your life'. On that basis, I could argue that I have been unemployed for more than 60 years now! I may have changed roles over the years, but my passion for the Club is still as strong as ever.

The *All-New Official Arsenal Miscellany* is a celebration of the traditions, visions and innovations of a Club at the forefront of world football. The first edition, full of interesting facts and stories, was immensely popular and inspired a wealth of copycat publications – you could say that Arsenal is once again creating the trends that other clubs will follow! This edition will, I hope, continue to intrigue, amaze and entertain Arsenal fans with its fascinating blend of trivia and tales from behind the scenes of one of the biggest and most successful football clubs in the world.

Ken Friar, Director, Arsenal Football Club

FOR STARTERS

Between them, Frank McLintock and Tony Adams played 1,072 games for Arsenal, captained the team to numerous trophies and became legends to the supporters in the process. However, each player had a difficult start to his Arsenal career.

Frank McLintock joined Arsenal in 1964 and made his debut against Nottingham Forest. During the match, McLintock misplaced a pass and the ball went straight to Forest's Arsenal old boy John Barnwell, who scored one of the goals in Forest's 3–0 victory.

Tony Adams made his Arsenal debut against Sunderland shortly after he turned 17. Understandably, the young debutant was a little nervous. However, it was only when the teams returned to the dressing room at half time that young Adams noticed his shorts were on the wrong way round.

POOR PAUL

During his first 14 matches against Arsenal, goalkeeper Paul Robinson conceded an astonishing 37 goals. The matches were:

26 November 2000 . . . . **Leeds United 1 Arsenal 0**
28 September 2002 . . . . **Leeds United 1 Arsenal 4**
4 May 2003 . . . . **Arsenal 2 Leeds United 3**
1 November 2003 . . . . **Leeds United 1 Arsenal 4**
4 January 2004 . . . . **Leeds United 1 Arsenal 4**
16 April 2004 . . . . **Arsenal 5 Leeds United 0**
13 November 2004 . . . . **Tottenham Hotspur 4 Arsenal 5**
25 April 2005 . . . . **Arsenal 1 Tottenham Hotspur 0**
29 October 2005 . . . . **Tottenham Hotspur 1 Arsenal 1**
22 April 2006 . . . . **Arsenal 1 Tottenham Hotspur 1**
2 December 2006 . . . . **Arsenal 3 Tottenham Hotspur 0**
24 January 2007 . . . . **Tottenham Hotspur 2 Arsenal 2**
31 January 2007 . . . . **Arsenal 3 Tottenham Hotspur 1**
21 April 2007 . . . . **Tottenham Hotspur 2 Arsenal 2**

HIGHBURY LANDMARKS

1913 .... Woolwich Arsenal plays its first match at Arsenal Stadium, Highbury and beats Leicester Fosse 2–1.

1925 .... The Club buys the stadium site outright.

1932 .... The West Stand is opened in December by HRH Prince of Wales. It has a 21,000 capacity.

1935 .... A roof is built over the Laundry End (later renamed the North Bank) and its clock installed at the front of the College End terrace, henceforth known as the Clock End.

1936 .... The Art Deco East Stand opens in October.

1939 .... Arsenal Stadium is turned into an Air Raid Precautions base for the duration of the Second World War.

1951 .... First official floodlit match (a friendly against Hapoel Tel Aviv).

1989 .... Executive boxes and roof over Clock End are erected.

1992 .... North Bank terrace is demolished to make way for a 12,500 seater two-tier North Bank Stand.

1993 .... North Bank Stand is reopened, making Highbury an all-seater stadium. Jumbotron screens are installed in the northwest and southeast corners of the stadium.

1999 .... The Club announces plans to move to a new stadium and Highbury's days are numbered.

2000 .... Highbury hosts its first ever UEFA Champions League match. Arsenal beat Shakhtar Donetsk 3–2.

2005 .... Arsenal's final game at the stadium playing in red and white is a romp as the Gunners beat Everton 7–0.

2006 .... In the final match ever played at Highbury, Arsenal beat Wigan Athletic 4–2 to seal fourth place in the Premiership at the expense of local rivals Tottenham Hotspur.

WENGER INNOVATIONS (1)

Training under Arsène Wenger became a whole new experience for the Arsenal players when he first arrived. Sessions were short and sharp and every activity was timed to the second by the stopwatch-brandishing Frenchman. Out went the distance runs and in came timed runs and bleep tests. Stretching was also introduced, including one session of stretching in a hotel ballroom prior to an away match against Blackburn Rovers.

ISLINGTON UNCOVERED (1)

Number 85 Avenell Road has now been demolished but, in 1903, it was used as a mailing address and safe house by a number of Russian Bolsheviks including Lenin.

THE THINGS THEY SAY

'Thirty years ago men went out with the fullest licence to display their arts and crafts. Today, they have to make their contributions to a system. Individuality has to be subordinated to team work. With us it is a case of goals and points. At times one is persuaded that nothing else matters.'

Herbert Chapman

BARGAIN BIRTHDAY

On the occasion of Arsène Wenger's tenth anniversary as Arsenal manager, the Club offered a 25 per cent discount on hand-filled pies and slashed prices for beer by 70p.

NUMBER CRUNCHING (1)

398 The number of matches it took for Arsène Wenger to collect 200 wins as Arsenal manager.

THE THINGS THEY SAY

*'It's Ian Wright, so good they named him thrice –
Ian Wright Wright Wright!'*

Commentator Jonathan Pearce announcing
one of Wright's goals for Arsenal

GOODBYE HIGHBURY

The final competitive match at Arsenal Stadium, Highbury:

7 May 2006 • Arsenal Stadium, Highbury • Attendance: 38,359
Arsenal 4 Wigan Athletic 2 (Goals: Pires 1, Henry 3)
Formation: 4-4-2

LEHMANN

EBOUE   TOURE   CAMPBELL   COLE

HLEB   FABREGAS   SILVA   PIRES

REYES   HENRY

Subs used: 11 van Persie (for Hleb), 10 Bergkamp (for Reyes),
8 Ljungberg (for Pires)

ARSENAL FANZINES

As with most football clubs there have been a fair few fanzines sold on the streets outside the Arsenal ground on matchday:

The Gooner
One-Nil Down, Two-One Up
Highbury High
Up the Arse
An Imperfect Match
On the Box
Arsenal Echo Echo
Highbury Wizard

On 20 November 1939, the Club wrote to season ticket holders outlining steps to be taken in recompensing them for matches they had paid to watch but that would not be taking place owing to the Second World War:

Dear Sir or Madam,

Season 1939/40

As you are already aware, football was suspended by Royal Proclamation on War being declared, with the result that only two First League Matches were able to be played at Highbury. Since then our Ground has been requisitioned by the Public Authorities.

You will appreciate the difficulties that confront the Club, as the present revenues are comparatively insignificant and may even cease entirely in the event of the continuation of hostilities. On the other hand, there is a considerable expenditure on overheads which must be met.

In these circumstances, the Directors, after most earnest consideration, have decided that Season Ticket Holders shall be granted free admission to all Regional Matches played by the Arsenal on the Tottenham Hotspur Football Ground for the duration of the War, or until further notice, and when normal League Football is resumed a new Season Ticket will be issued for the whole of the first season in exchange for the present ticket. No further charge will be made and so far as possible the same seat or seats as those previously booked will be allotted.

It is to be hoped that this arrangement will commend itself to you, and I look forward to the time when all Arsenal supporters will be able to foregather on the Highbury Ground as they have done in the past.

Yours faithfully,

George Allison,
Secretary Manager

BORING, BORING ARSENAL (1)

Arsenal scored ten goals in one round of their successful European Cup Winners' Cup campaign in 1993/94. The unfortunate opponents were Standard Liege of Belgium. Having beaten them 3–0 at Highbury in the first leg, the Gunners thrashed them 7–0 in the second leg in Belgium.

EMIRATES EXCELLENCE (1)

Sir Robert McAlpine Ltd was appointed to build the new stadium. McAlpine has previously built the Millennium Dome, the new Hampden Park Stadium in Glasgow and the Centenary Stand at West Ham United's Upton Park.

DID YOU KNOW?

Arsenal won the title in the 1937/38 season and somehow managed to score fewer goals during the campaign than Manchester City, who were relegated that same season!

TRUMPING THE CHAMPS

Two of Arsenal's League Championships were secured when the Gunners beat the defending champions on their own turf. The matches were Arsenal's 2–0 victory over Liverpool at Anfield in 1989 and the 1–0 victory over Manchester United at Old Trafford in 2002.

DAVID'S DERBIES

David Platt appeared in five separate derby matches during his football career:

Crewe v Chester City
Aston Villa v Birmingham
Juventus v Torino
Sampdoria v Genoa
Arsenal v Tottenham Hotspur

COMPTON LOSES A CAP

In 1938, Denis Compton damaged his knee in a collision with an opposing goalkeeper and his subsequent sporting career on both the cricket and football fields was seriously afflicted by knee problems. Eventually, in November 1955, he underwent surgery to have his right kneecap removed. The surgeon kept the kneecap as a souvenir and later donated it to Middlesex County Cricket Club as a part of their Lord's archive. It has been described as looking like a medium-sized mushroom, honey-coloured and honey-combed.

WAR!

'Cancel close-season game in Germany.'

Arsenal FC board meeting minutes, *13 April 1939*

JIM'LL FIX IT

In 1980, the British Heart Foundation wrote a letter to Jimmy Savile of the BBC's *Jim'll Fix It* programme on behalf of a team of young boys who had undergone heart surgery. In response to the letter, the team were invited to play at Arsenal Stadium against an Arsenal side. In January 1981, Heart Line – the name given to the young boys' team – faced a Gunners side that included Pat Jennings, John Hollins, Kenny Sansom, David O'Leary and Frank Stapleton.

The Arsenal team won the friendly 5–4, prompting the headline 'Hearts 4, Arsenal 5' in the *Sunday Mirror*. Twelve members of the Heart Line team returned to the Stadium 25 years on, as part of the Club's final season celebrations at Highbury.

DID YOU KNOW?

Former Arsenal midfielder Stewart Robson went to the same school as television presenter Noel Edmonds (Brentwood). England midfielder Frank Lampard also attended.

THE LAST FOUR (1)

Arsenal have played in 12 League Cup semi-finals. As the semi-finals in the competition are always played over two legs, this constitutes 25 matches, including one replay:

17 January 1968 .... **Arsenal 3 Huddersfield Town 2**
6 February 1968 .... **Huddersfield Town 1 Arsenal 3**
(Arsenal lost the Final 1–0 to Leeds United)

20 November 1968 .... **Arsenal 1 Tottenham Hotspur 0**
4 December 1968 ...... **Tottenham Hotspur 1 Arsenal 1**
(Arsenal lost the Final 3–1 to Swindon Town)

7 February 1978 .... **Liverpool 2 Arsenal 1**
14 February 1978 .... **Arsenal 0 Liverpool 0**

15 February 1983 ...... **Arsenal 2 Manchester United 4**
22 February 1983 ...... **Manchester United 2 Arsenal 1**

8 February 1987 .... **Arsenal 0 Tottenham Hotspur 1**
1 March 1987 .... **Tottenham Hotspur 1 Arsenal 2**
4 March 1987 .... **Tottenham Hotspur 1 Arsenal 2**
(Arsenal beat Liverpool 2–1 in the Final)

7 February 1988 .... **Everton 0 Arsenal 1**
24 February 1988 .... **Arsenal 3 Everton 1**
(Arsenal lost the Final 3–2 to Luton Town)

7 February 1993 .... **Crystal Palace 1 Arsenal 3**
10 March 1993 .... **Arsenal 2 Crystal Palace 0**
(Arsenal beat Sheffield Wednesday 2–1 in the Final)

14 February 1996 .... **Arsenal 2 Aston Villa 2**
21 February 1996 .... **Aston Villa 0 Arsenal 0**

28 January 1998 .... **Arsenal 2 Chelsea 1**
18 February 1998 .... **Chelsea 3 Arsenal 1**

20 January 2004 .... **Arsenal 0 Middlesbrough 1**
3 February 2004 .... **Middlesbrough 2 Arsenal 1**

| 10 January 2006 . . . . | **Wigan Athletic 1 Arsenal 0** |
| 24 January 2006 . . . . | **Arsenal 2 Wigan Athletic 1** |

| 17 January 2007 . . . . . . | **Tottenham Hotspur 2 Arsenal 2** |
| 31 January 2007 . . . . | **Arsenal 3 Tottenham Hotspur 1** |

(Arsenal lost the Final 2–1 to Chelsea)

Overall record

Pld	W	D	L	F	A
25	**12**	**5**	**8**	**37**	**31**

HAT-TRICKS ON THE BRAIN

Doug Lishman has rightly received praise for scoring hat-tricks in three consecutive home games for Arsenal during the 1951/52 season. However, he is not the only Gunner to achieve this feat. During the 1925/26 season, Jimmy Brain also hit three goals in three consecutive home games:

17 October 1925	**Arsenal 5 Cardiff City 0**
31 October 1925	**Arsenal 4 Everton 1**
14 November 1925	**Arsenal 6 Bury 1**

In addition, Jimmy hit another hat-trick later that season when Arsenal beat Everton away 3–2.

ANDERS ASSISTS

When Arsenal beat Everton 4–2 on 21 December 1991, Ian Wright scored all four goals and Anders Limpar set up each and every one of them.

ISLINGTON UNCOVERED (2)

Charles Cruft, founder of the famous dog show that takes his name, lived on Highbury Grove between 1913 and 1938.

LUCKY ARSENAL?

Arsenal has long had to bear the accusation that they are 'lucky'. As far back as the 1950s, the Club has defended itself against this claim. The following extract comes from a publication called *Voice of Arsenal* from 3 May 1950, produced shortly after the team won the FA Cup, beating Liverpool 2–0 in the Final:

> *'What of that term, Lucky Arsenal which has been heard too often in recent times and particularly during this season's cup exploits? The cry went up with each home draw, when we beat 10-man Sheffield Wednesday in the Third Round, again when Swansea Town, Burnley, Leeds were defeated. And, as was to be expected, it was shouted from the house-tops after Freddie Cox's corkscrew goal against Chelsea. Well, we will say 'Thanks Lady Luck' for whatever assistance she gave, but at the same time we will continue to believe that somehow Joe Mercer and the team had something to do with our reaching Wembley!'*

SVEN'S HIGHBURY GAMES

Former England manager Sven-Goran Eriksson was the manager of a visiting team at Highbury on three occasions in competitive matches. He won one of these ties and was on the losing side twice:

5 March 1980 . . . . **Arsenal 5 IFK Gothenburg 1**
European Cup Winners' Cup, quarter-final, first leg

6 November 1991 . . . . **Arsenal 1 Benfica 3**
European Cup, second round, second leg

6 April 1995 . . . . **Arsenal 3 Sampdoria 2**
European Cup Winners' Cup semi-final, first leg

Eriksson was also the manager of Sampdoria when the Italians were the guests for Alan Smith's testimonial match in November 1995. Arsenal won the friendly 2–0.

TRIBUTE TO HERBERT CHAPMAN

Extracts from the Vicar Of Hendon's tribute to Herbert Chapman. The Vicar presided over Chapman's funeral.

'It is very, very seldom that the death of any person calls forth such spontaneous and widespread grief as did the sudden death of Herbert Chapman when it was announced in the early editions of the evening papers on Saturday last.

'A doctor in the north of England, writing to me on the following day on quite other matters, had this sentence in his letter: "Yesterday was a day of gloom here because of Chapman's death." And that is just typical of the feelings of thousands quite unknown personally to Mr Chapman, and far removed from any connection with the doings of the Club that he had helped to make so famous.

'A Naval officer told me how, when he was in command of one of His Majesty's ships in far distant waters, on what corresponds to a Saturday evening in London, a signalman would come to him in his cabin with a signal pad in his hand and a smile on his face. "What is it?" the officer would say. "Arsenal won, Sir", the sailor would reply.

'No doubt Mr Chapman's interest in, and connection with, Hendon Parish Church were well known to his more intimate acquaintances. For he was very fond of this church and very proud of it and he must often have spoken of it to friends. But of the tens and thousands who have thought of him as a man wholly absorbed in football there will be many who will learn with surprise that for many years Mr Chapman has held office here as a sidesman, and Sunday by Sunday, if duty did not call him away from Hendon, was to be found either at the morning or evening service as the case may be.

'The general public mourns a great sportsman. Football mourns a genius. The Church mourns a faithful and devoted son and commends his soul to God.'

PARK LIFE

The official car park for Arsenal reserves matches at Barnet's Underhill ground is the car park at High Barnet underground station.

GREAT GOALS (1)

Sylvain Wiltord
8 May 2002 • Manchester United 0 Arsenal 1
Premiership, Old Trafford

This was the match that sealed the title in 2001/02 and confirmed the Gunners – who had beaten Chelsea in the FA Cup Final only days earlier – as winners of the Double. In the 57th minute, Mikael Silvestre conceded possession to Sylvain Wiltord, who released the ball into the path of Freddie Ljungberg. The Swede beat Laurent Blanc but his shot was parried by Fabien Barthez. Wiltord met the loose ball and fired home. Arsenal only needed a draw in this tie but Wiltord's goal made sure Arsenal won both the match and the title.

DID YOU KNOW?

Viewers in 115 countries worldwide watched Arsenal beat Chelsea 2–0 in the 2002 FA Cup Final.

SIXES AND SEVENS

- The 6–6 draw with Leicester City in 1930 is the joint largest draw in top-flight English football. (Charlton Athletic also drew 6–6 with Middlesbrough on 22 October 1960.)

- Arsenal's 6–0 win at White Hart Lane in 1935 is the biggest ever north London Derby victory.

- Ted Drake scored all seven of Arsenal's goals away to Aston Villa in 1935. An individual top-flight record that still stands today.

- In Arsenal's 6–2 win at Villa Park in 1983, five of the goals were scored by Tony Woodcock.

- The Gunners recorded two 7–0 victories at Highbury in eight months. In May 2005, they thrashed Everton 7–0 and then repeated that scoreline at home to Middlesbrough in January 2006.

- When Arsenal beat Liverpool 6–3 at Anfield in the League Cup, January 2007, this was the first time they had scored six goals in an away match since beating Queen's Park Rangers 6–0 at Loftus Road in the fourth round of the 2001 FA Cup.

24 February 1894	**Middlesbrough Ironopolis 3 Arsenal 6**	League
21 April 1930	**Leicester City 6 Arsenal 6**	League
5 February 1931	**Leicester City 2 Arsenal 7**	League
5 November 1932	**Wolverhampton Wanderers 1 Arsenal 7**	League
6 March 1935	**Tottenham Hotspur 0 Arsenal 6**	League
14 December 1935	**Aston Villa 1 Arsenal 7**	League
20 February 1937	**Burnley 1 Arsenal 7**	FA Cup
25 December 1952	**Bolton Wanderers 4 Arsenal 6**	League
6 September 1958	**Everton 1 Arsenal 6**	League
25 September 1963	**Staevnet Copenhagen 1 Arsenal 7**	Fairs Cup
25 September 1968	**Scunthorpe United 1 Arsenal 6**	League Cup
29 October 1983	**Aston Villa 2 Arsenal 6**	League
3 October 1989	**Plymouth Argyle 1 Arsenal 6**	League Cup
3 November 1993	**Standard Liege 0 Arsenal 7**	European Cup Winners' Cup
24 April 1999	**Middlesbrough 1 Arsenal 6**	League
27 January 2001	**QPR 0 Arsenal 6**	FA Cup
11 May 2005	**Arsenal 7 Everton 0**	Premiership
14 January 2006	**Arsenal 7 Middlesbrough 0**	Premiership
23 December 2006	**Arsenal 6 Blackburn Rovers 2**	Premiership
9 January 2007	**Liverpool 3 Arsenal 6**	League Cup

HAT-TRICKS AGAINST HOTSPUR

Two Arsenal players have scored hat-tricks against Tottenham Hotspur:

Ted Drake
20 October 1934 **Arsenal 5 Tottenham Hotspur 1**

Alan Sunderland
23 December 1978 **Tottenham Hotspur 0 Arsenal 5**

BOARDROOM POLITICS

The first directors of Arsenal Football Club were appointed during the 1890s. The first set of directors included a surgeon, a coffee-house owner, a builder and six engineers.

UNHAPPY RETURNS

During the Club's stay at Highbury, a former Arsenal player returned to the ground with his new team on two occasions in European competition. On both occasions, it was an unhappy return for the former Gunner.

Silvinho, who played for Arsenal between 1999 and 2001, returned with Celta Vigo in the UEFA Champions League in 2004. Arsenal won the first knockout-round second-leg match 2–0, to progress 5–2 on aggregate.

Patrick Vieira, who was an Arsenal player between 1996 and 2005, was in the Juventus line-up that faced Arsenal at Highbury on 28 March 2006. The Gunners won the UEFA Champions League quarter-final first leg 2–0 and then drew 0–0 in the second leg in Italy to reach the semi-final of the competition.

HAT-TRICK FACTS

During the 1930/31 season, Arsenal players scored 12 hat-tricks during the 42 games. Jack Lambert scored three of those hat-tricks in one month and seven overall. The other hat-tricks that season came from David Jack (3), Cliff Bastin (1) and Jimmy Brain (1).

MILJAN MANAGER?

Twenty years before Arsène Wenger became manager, Arsenal almost appointed another European for the big job – Serbian Miljan Miljanic, then manager of Real Madrid. He was very heavily tipped to replace outgoing boss, Bertie Mee.

Chairman Denis Hill-Wood said: 'His record, of course, is superb and during the two half-hour sessions we had in Madrid, he struck me as being an outstanding type of man. Just as I'd been told, he's a strong, healthy, clean-looking man. Providing everything works out, he will simply take over Bertie Mee's role.'

However, captain Alan Ball was less enthused. He said: 'The new manager will arrive here as a complete stranger and my guess is that it will take him a year to settle in. I feel choked for Bobby Campbell, our coach. They should have given the job to him in the first place.'

As it turned out, of course, Terry Neill got the job.

OTHER PEOPLE CALLED ARSÈNE

- **Arsène Lupin** A fictional character appearing in the works of French crime stories by Maurice Leblanc
- **Arsène Oka** A footballer from Ivory Coast currently playing in the Major League Soccer (MLS) in the US
- **Arsène James** A St Lucian politician
- **Arsène Houssaye** A 19th-century French novelist and poet
- **Arsène Roux** A 20th-century language expert

THE THINGS THEY SAY

'5–2 is too cavalier. I would have preferred 2–0 or 3–0.'

George Graham following the home victory
over Sheffield United, *1991*

BOBBY'S DERBY DELIGHT

Robert Pires spent six years as an Arsenal player. During that time he scored against local rivals Tottenham Hotspur on eight occasions:

31 March 2001 . . . . . . **Arsenal 2 Tottenham Hotspur 0** . Premiership
8 April 2001 . . . . **Tottenham Hotspur 1 Arsenal 2** . . . . . . FA Cup
17 November 2001 . . **Tottenham Hotspur 1 Arsenal 1** . Premiership
15 December 2002 . . **Tottenham Hotspur 1 Arsenal 1** . . Premiership
8 November 2003 . . . **Arsenal 2 Tottenham Hotspur 1** . Premiership
25 April 2004 . . . . . . **Tottenham Hotspur 2 Arsenal 2** . Premiership
13 November 2004 . . **Tottenham Hotspur 4 Arsenal 5** . Premiership
29 October 2005 . . . . **Tottenham Hotspur 1 Arsenal 1** . . Premiership

HIGHBURY – WHAT HAPPENED NEXT?

Arsenal moved from Highbury Stadium to Emirates Stadium in the summer of 2006. Here is the future of Highbury:

- The East and West Stand façades have been retained.

- The famous marble entrance hall in the East Stand is the arrival area for the whole development.

- The Art Deco West Stand is being converted into 116 studio flats, a mixture of one-bedroom, two-bedroom and three-bedroom apartments.

- The North and South Stands have been replaced by apartment buildings.

- There will be two acres of gardens on the former pitch, landscaped in the style of a typical London square.

CH..CH..CH..CHANGES

In January 2006, *Four Four Two* magazine named 'The six men who changed football', and devoted a title cover to each of the men. The six 'men' were Jean Marc Bosman, Eric Cantona, David Beckham, Roman Abramovich, Sky Television and Arsène Wenger.

A small selection of clauses from the 2005 Arsenal Football Club Charter:

Accessibility
The Club continues to strive for wider spectator access to matches by offering half-price admission for disabled supporters and free admission for their carers.

Away support
The Club does not charge admission prices to supporters of a visiting club that are higher than those charged to our own supporters for comparable accommodation.

Consultation and information
Since season 2001/02, the Club has hosted regular 'Fans Forums'. Seventeen supporters attend four forums per season and represent different supporter groups by discussing various issues with senior members of the administration team and the Club's Managing Director.

Community activity
The Community Department is committed to offering a range of sporting, social inclusion, educational and charitable projects; the success of which is testament to the commitment and dedication of its staff and the power of football and Arsenal Football Club to touch people's lives on a local, regional and global scale.

Good causes policy
Arsenal Football Club is committed to offering its support to charitable projects and good causes wherever possible. Primarily, the Club will offer support to requests from the local community, with particular focus upon initiatives operating within the Islington area.

Merchandise
The Club will consider its traditional values, along with commercial considerations, when producing new playing strips.

The Stadium
The Club endeavours to ensure that Emirates Stadium is maintained to the highest standards ensuring that it is a safe, functional and pleasant environment for supporters and all other users.

EMIRATES EXCELLENCE (2)

Over 60,000 cubic metres (2,119,000 cubic feet) of concrete were used to build Emirates Stadium. About 10,000 tonnes of steel reinforcement were used. Over 3,000 tonnes of tubular steel were used in the main roof – compared to just 100 tonnes used in Highbury's North Bank.

THE ARSENAL BOARD 2006/07

Peter Hill-Wood **Chairman**
Keith Edelman **Managing Director**
Richard Carr **Director**
Daniel Fiszman **Director**
Ken Friar OBE **Director**
Sir Chips Keswick **Director**
Lord Harris of Peckham **Director**
Lady Nina Bracewell-Smith **Director**
Clive Carr **Life Vice-president**

TERRIFIC THIERRY (1)

In the 2005/06 season, Thierry Henry scored more goals than the entire Sunderland AFC team managed in the same campaign. Henry scored 27 times, the Sunderland team scored just 26 between them.

THE THINGS THEY SAY

'I feel wound up for today's event.
Tell people who suggest my playing career is over that
I am not thinking of finishing with football.'

Alex James, prior to Arsenal's 1936 FA Cup Final victory
over Sheffield United

PLAYER OF THE MONTH

A year in the life of the arsenal.com Player of the Month award:

August 2005	**Alexander Hleb**
September 2005	**Sol Campbell**
October 2005	**Thierry Henry**
November 2005	**Robin van Persie**
December 2005	**Jose Antonio Reyes**
January 2006	**Thierry Henry**
February 2006	**Jens Lehmann**
March 2006	**Cesc Fabregas**
April 2006	**Jens Lehmann**
May 2006	**Thierry Henry** (player of the season)
August 2006	**Cesc Fabregas**

GOALSCORING GOALKEEPERS

Two Arsenal goalkeepers scored for their previous clubs:

Playing for Tottenham Hotspur in 1967, **Pat Jennings** launched a powerful drop kick from his own area during the Charity Shield match against Manchester United. The ball flew towards his opposite number, Alex Stepney, but the United goalkeeper misjudged the bounce of the ball and it flew over him and into the net. The previous time that a goalkeeper had scored direct from a goal kick in England was in 1900, when Manchester City's Charlie Williams was the scorer against Sunderland.

On 19 December 1997, **Jens Lehmann** scored a late equalizer for Schalke 04 against local rivals Borussia Dortmund. It was a controversial strike for a number of reasons: the awarding of the preceding corner kick had been hotly disputed by Borussia Dortmund; and it was claimed that Lehmann was in an offside position when he scored. However, the goal stood and earned his team a 2–2 draw. Lehmann later joined Borussia Dortmund.

DID YOU KNOW?

**Arsenal topped the Barclays Premiership Fair Play League for
two successive seasons, in 2003/04 and 2004/05.**

SECRETS OF THE 1947/48 CHAMPIONSHIP TEAM

George Male

'I enjoy doing a little gardening or painting at home, or lecturing at youth clubs. I smoke a pipe and, among my team mates, have something of a reputation for being a big eater.'

Walley Barnes

'I smoke very little and my favourite meal is filleted plaice, fried as only my mother-in-law can do it.'

Leslie Compton

'Smoking has no attraction for me and only rarely do I have an odd glass of beer.'

Archie Macaulay

'During training I limit myself to eight cigarettes daily and keep off intoxicants. I enjoy my wife's Scottish cooking more than the best hotel food.'

Bryn Jones

'As for grub, give me a steak and chips and you can keep the rest.'

Reg Lewis

'I smoke in moderation, drink very little and have no fads about eating. When I can get it, I never refuse a nice juicy steak and chips.'

Joe Mercer

'I'm sorry, but I've no startling confessions to make.'

IT'S THEM AGAIN

In January 2007, Arsenal met in two cup ties in four days at Anfield. The first came on Saturday 6 January in the FA Cup third round, the second came on Tuesday 9 January in the League Cup quarter-final. Arsenal won the first match 3–1 and returned to win the second game 6–3.

SO GOOD THEY DID IT TWICE

It's always nice to beat Tottenham Hotspur! So it was doubly nice to beat them twice in eight days in 2001.

Arsenal 2 Tottenham Hotspur 0
31 March 2001
Premiership
Goals: Pires (70), Henry (87)

Arsenal 2 Tottenham Hotspur 1
8 April 2001
FA Cup semi-final (at Old Trafford)
Goals: Vieira (33), Pires (74)

THE 49-MATCH UNBEATEN RUN (1)

- The 49-match unbeaten run started on Wednesday 7 May 2003 with a 6–1 defeat of Southampton.
- Thirty-six of the 49 matches were victories and there were 13 draws, four of them goalless.
- The Gunners amassed 121 points during the 49 matches.
- The team scored 112 goals and conceded just 35 during the run.
- Five own goals were included among the 112 goals the team notched up.
- The Club used a total of 33 different players during the unbeaten League season.
- Fifteen different Arsenal players scored during the run.
- Thierry Henry scored 39 times during the 49 games, while Robert Pires found the back of the net 23 times.

WENGER INNOVATIONS (2)

In 1998, the Arsenal Academy was set up under Wenger's watchful eye as the Club became one of the first in England to get academy status. Since then, Wenger has turned the League Cup into a testing ground for young players. It has proved rewarding: not only have the likes of Cesc Fabregas, Justin Hoyte and Jeremie Aliadiere emerged into the first team after such bloodings, the Club reached the League Cup semi-final in 2006 and the Final in 2007.

THE SPOTLESS SPOT-KICK RECORD

England have exited five international tournaments following a penalty shoot-out since 1990. Arsenal is the only English club whose players have a 100 per cent success record during these shoot-outs. David Platt (Euro 96) and Ashley Cole (Euro 2004) both took and scored spot-kicks as Arsenal players. In addition, Platt took a spot-kick before becoming an Arsenal player (World Cup 1990) and Paul Merson took one after leaving the Club (World Cup 1998).

The only other English clubs whose players have never missed are Blackburn Rovers, Middlesbrough and Tottenham Hotspur but their records are sullied by misses from former or future players.

1990

Gary Lineker (Tottenham Hotspur) .... scored
Peter Beardsley (Liverpool) .... scored
David Platt (Aston Villa) .... scored
Stuart Pearce (Nottingham Forest) .... missed
Chris Waddle (Marseille) .... missed

1996

Alan Shearer (Blackburn Rovers) .... scored
David Platt (Arsenal) .... scored
Stuart Pearce (Nottingham Forest) .... scored
Paul Gascoigne (Rangers) .... scored
Teddy Sheringham (Tottenham Hotspur) .... scored
Gareth Southgate (Aston Villa) .... missed

1998

Alan Shearer (Newcastle United) .... scored
Paul Ince (Liverpool) .... missed
Paul Merson (Middlesbrough) .... scored
Michael Owen (Liverpool) .... scored
David Batty (Newcastle United) .... missed

2004

David Beckham (Real Madrid) .... missed
Michael Owen (Liverpool) .... scored
Frank Lampard (Chelsea) .... scored
John Terry (Chelsea) .... scored

Owen Hargreaves (Bayern Munich) .... scored
Ashley Cole (Arsenal) .... scored
Darius Vassell (Aston Villa) .... missed

2006

Frank Lampard (Chelsea) .... missed
Owen Hargreaves (Bayern Munich) .... scored
Steven Gerrard (Liverpool) .... missed
Jamie Carragher (Liverpool) .... missed

THE LEGENDS HAD IT

For the second half of Dennis Bergkamp's testimonial match on 22 July 2006, the two clubs – Arsenal and Ajax – fielded teams made up by legends past and present. The two squads were:

Arsenal Legends	Ajax Legends
David Seaman	Edwin van der Sar
Lee Dixon	Stanley Menzo
Nigel Winterburn	Danny Blind
Steve Bould	Wim Jonk
Gilles Grimandi	Frank De Boer
Marc Overmars	Marciano Vink
Emmanuel Petit	Aron Winter
Edu	Ronald de Boer
Ray Parlour	Edgar Davids
Dennis Bergkamp	Jan Wouters
Thierry Henry	Stefan Pettersson
Ian Wright	Bryan Roy
Oleg Luzhny	Johan Cruyff
Giovanni van Bronckhorst	Frank Rijkaard
Alex Manninger	Marco van Basten
Patrick Vieira	
Glenn Helder	
Nwankwo Kanu	

THE FINAL MATCH PLAYED IN FRONT
OF A STANDING NORTH BANK

Rarely can an end-of-season defeat of the Southampton team in a non-championship-winning campaign have proved to be such a poignant and significant affair. This was the final match played in front of a standing North Bank. Ian Wright's hat-trick meant he beat Tottenham's Gary Lineker to the Golden Boot at the last hurdle.* This was also David Rocastle's final match for the Club.

FOOTBALL LEAGUE DIVISION ONE
2 May 1992 • Arsenal Stadium, Highbury • Attendance: 37,702
Arsenal 5 Southampton 1 (Goals: Campbell 1, Smith 1, Wright 3)
Formation: 4-4-2

SEAMAN

 DIXON   BOULD   ADAMS   WINTERBURN

 LIMPAR   HILLIER   MERSON   ROCASTLE

 WRIGHT   CAMPBELL

Subs used: 9 Smith (for Limpar), 15 Parlour (for Merson)

That summer, another Arsenal striker denied Gary Lineker a further record. In what proved to be his final England match, the Tottenham striker was one goal away from equalling Bobby Charlton's England goalscoring record when manager Graham Taylor substituted him in favour of Alan Smith in the group game against Sweden.

MAGIC NUMBERS: 10 OUT OF 10

- Arsène Wenger said: 'It will take around ten games until Emirates Stadium feels like home.' The tenth game was a Premiership clash with Newcastle United, which ended in a 1–1 draw.

- Arsenal won their sixth League Championship on 10 April 1948.

- In closing in on the 1997/98 League title, Arsenal won ten straight Premiership games from the 1–0 victory over Wimbledon on 11 March 1998 to the decisive 4–0 victory over Everton on 3 May 1998.

- When Arsenal lifted the Premiership trophy that day, Francesc Fabregas was spending his last day as a ten-year-old.

- Arsenal scored ten goals on aggregate against Standard Liege in their victorious run during the 1993/94 European Cup Winners' Cup campaign.

- Arsenal legends Charlie George and Tony Adams were both born on 10 October (1950 and 1966 respectively).

- When Paul Merson was asked if he would surrender his number 10 shirt to new signing Dennis Bergkamp, he replied: 'Blimey, it's Dennis Bergkamp – no problem!'

- Following the final competitive match at Highbury, Arsène Wenger led the supporters in counting down the final ten seconds of the Highbury countdown clock.

- Bertie Mee spent ten years as Arsenal manager between 1966 and 1976.

- Arsenal scored ten goals in all competitions in October 2006.

THE THINGS THEY SAY

*'Winning isn't just about pretty football.
It's about hunger – application.'*

George Graham, *August 1993*

FOLLOWING FORTUNES

Although Arsenal were unable to repeat their 1998 League Championship triumph the following season, the statistics show that they won the same points in both campaigns and actually lost fewer games and conceded fewer goals in the 1998/99 season.

	Pld	W	D	L	F	A	Pts
1997/98	38	23	9	6	68	33	78
1998/99	38	22	12	4	59	17	78

PATRICK GALLIGAN – A TRIBUTE

Patrick Galligan, who died in July 2006, had been on the Arsenal ground-staff for nearly three decades. Paddy, as he was known, joined the Club's general maintenance staff in 1976, having previously worked for the company that installed the seating in the lower tier of the West Stand. He was 'talent spotted', eventually to become the man who looked after both the home and the visitors' dressing rooms. Paddy became part of the fabric of the Club of which he was so proud and which he loved dearly.

Charlie George said: 'Everyone knew Paddy and everyone liked him because he'd do anything for anyone and the Club just won't be the same without him.' Lee Dixon added: 'He loved the Club so much, Mr Arsenal you could say, and we'll all miss him.' A Club statement said: 'He will not be forgotten by all of those that were privileged to know him, and we extend to his children, Johanna, Patrick and David, the very sincere condolences from the Directors, players and staff of "his Club".'

Before the home match with Aston Villa on 19 August 2006, there was a period of applause in tribute to him.

DID YOU KNOW?

When Arsenal lost 2–0 to Manchester United on 7 December 2002, it was the first time that the Gunners had failed to score in 56 matches.

QUICK CUP FACTS

- In the victorious 1970/71 FA Cup campaign, Arsenal were not drawn at home once. However, two of their ties – Portsmouth in the fourth round and Leicester in the sixth round – ended in draws, which meant the ties had to be replayed at Highbury.

- Arsenal were the first team to win both the FA Cup and the League Cup in the same year – 1993 – beating Sheffield Wednesday on both of the occasions.

- Arsène Wenger is the only Arsenal manager to win the FA Cup more than once.

- Mr Wenger also led Arsenal to five successive FA Cup semi-finals between 2001 and 2005.

- At least one team among Arsenal, Manchester United, Chelsea and Liverpool appeared in the FA Cup Final between 1992 and 2007.

- Freddie Ljungberg scored in two consecutive FA Cup Finals: the 2001 2–1 defeat by Liverpool and the 2002 2–0 victory over Chelsea.

- Patrick Vieira appeared in eight semi-finals for Arsenal including the 1999 replay. Freddie Ljungberg has appeared in seven.

- Emmet Smith runs RH Wilkins, which was the FA's official engravers while the Cup Final was played at the Millennium Stadium. As an Arsenal fan, he was delighted to be able to engrave the Club's name on the trophy three times.

FREEDOM

On 28 October 2004, Arsenal manager Arsène Wenger and Club director Ken Friar were awarded the Freedom of the Borough of Islington. This honour – the highest a local authority can bestow – was in recognition of the pair's outstanding service to the people and Borough of Islington. Both men became honorary freepersons of the Borough and were given a framed, hand-painted scroll at the special ceremony at Islington Town Hall.

First squad

The first-team squad that Wenger inherited when he took the reigns at Arsenal was: David Seaman, John Lukic, Vince Bartram, Lee Dixon, Gavin McGowan, Stephen Morrow, Nigel Winterburn, Tony Adams, Steve Bould, Martin Keown, Andy Linighan, Scott Marshall, Matthew Rose, David Hillier, Ian Selley, David Platt, Ray Parlour, Eddie McGoldrick, Paul Shaw, Stephen Hughes, Patrick Vieira, Remi Garde, Adrian Clarke, Glenn Helder, Paul Merson, Dennis Bergkamp, Ian Wright, John Hartson, Chris Kiwomya and Paul Dickov.

First game

As Mr Wenger's contract started on 1 October 1996, his first official game in charge was away to Blackburn Rovers on 12 October. Arsenal won 2–0 with both goals coming from Ian Wright. The team that day was:

Subs used: 15 Parlour (for Hartson)
Subs not used: 12 Linighan, 18 Morrow, 24 Lukic, 27 Shaw.
Attendance: 24, 303 • Referee: S Dunn • Booked: Hartson, Keown

First home game

On the following Saturday came Arsène's first home game, against Coventry City on 19 October. The game ended goalless but the point they earned lifted the Gunners to the top of the table. The team was:

SEAMAN

DIXON   KEOWN   ADAMS   BOULD   WINTERBURN

VIEIRA   PLATT   MERSON

HARTSON   WRIGHT

Subs used: 10 Bergkamp (for Hartson)
Subs not used: 15 Parlour, 18 Morrow, 19 Garde, 24 Lukic.
Attendance: 38,140 • Referee: P Jones • Booked: Hartson,
Wright, Keown

THE THINGS THEY SAY

'There's no chance of Sol leaving for Arsenal.
He is a Spurs fan and there's not a hope in hell of him
playing in an Arsenal shirt.'

David Buchler, Tottenham Hotspur Vice-chairman, *2001*

DID YOU KNOW?

Theo Walcott did not make his Arsenal debut until seven months
after he had joined the Club.

BBC SPORTS PERSONALITY OF THE YEAR

Arsenal personnel have won four awards at the
BBC Sports Personality of the Year bashes:

Arsenal FC **Team of the Year** 1998
Arsène Wenger **Coach of the Year** 2002, 2004
Theo Walcott **Young Personality of the Year** 2006

PIZZA EXCESS

A quick look at past and present Arsenal players' favourite toppings:

Patrick Vieira **Pepperoni**
Sebastian Larsson **Ham and Beef**
Alexandre Song **Bolognese**
Theo Walcott **Four cheese**
Robert Pires **Mushrooms, egg and ham**

BORING, BORING ARSENAL (2)

The Gunners scored in 27 consecutive away matches in a glorious run
that spanned the 2001/02 and 2002/03 seasons.

WILD ABOUT THE ROVERS (1)

During the Club's 1997/98 Premiership-winning campaign, Blackburn
Rovers proved to be significant opponents. On 13 December 1997,
Arsenal lost 3–1 to Blackburn Rovers at Highbury. In the wake of this
defeat – which left the Gunners languishing mid-table – the team held a
special meeting at their training base. Following the meeting, the team
did not lose another match until the title had been secured with a 4–0
victory at home to Everton. A key victory in that unbeaten run was the 4–1
victory away to Ewood Park on 13 April 1998.

BY GEORGE!

Of the 19 managers Arsenal have had during its history, five have been called George: George Elcoat, George Morrell, George Allison, George Swindin and George Graham. This means that if you have managed the Club, you have a 26.3 per cent chance of being called George. Additionally, the trainer of the 1914/15 side was called George Hardy.

Two of the managers named George (Messrs Swindin and Graham) also played for Arsenal. As well as these two, there have been a number of other Georges in Arsenal's playing history including: George Grant (1911–14), George Ford (1912–15), George Male (1930–48), George Eastham (1960–66), George Armstrong (1961–77), George Johnston (1967–69) Charlie George (1969–75), George Wood (1980–83).

SEEING RED

The first red card shown at Emirates Stadium came during the 1–1 draw with Middlesbrough on 9 September 2006. Boro's George Boateng was the recipient.

SOUR SUGAR

Alan Sugar is now most famous for his appearances on the television show *The Apprentice*, complete with his famous catchphrase: 'You're fired!' However, he was once the chairman of Tottenham Hotspur.

While at White Hart Lane he discussed a new Arsenal signing with the press. 'It's total madness,' he said, adding, 'If Bergkamp thinks he's going to set the world alight, he can forget it. He is a good player but he won't be successful. Arsenal got him because they needed a bit of cosmetic marketing.'

Dennis Bergkamp stayed with the Club for 11 years, scoring 120 goals in 423 appearances. Not a bad piece of cosmetic marketing!

Mind you, Sugar was not alone in predicting poor fortunes for Bergkamp. President of Inter Milan, Massimo Moratti, said: 'Arsenal will be lucky if Bergkamp scores ten goals this season.'

TURN UP THE HEAT

The winter of 1962–63 was a particularly harsh one. On Boxing Day, Highbury was covered in a blanket of snow and there were 3-metre (10-feet) deep drifts on the terraces. After the home match against Leyton Orient on 15 December 1962, the Club did not play again at Highbury until 30 January 1963. The following year, the Club installed under-soil heating beneath the pitch for the first time. It cost the Club £15,000 to cut trenches into the pitch and insert a total of 50 km (31 miles) of electric cables. Six years later, the Club installed an improved under-soil heating system at a cost of £30,000.

GEORGE'S JUDGEMENT

When he arrived at Arsenal, in 1960, following a protracted transfer saga, George Eastham scored twice and starred during a 5–1 victory for the Gunners. This proved that he had been worth waiting for.

The delay in his joining Arsenal had been caused by a dispute that Eastham had with his former club Newcastle United. In December 1959 he had refused to sign a new contract because he wished to move elsewhere. Newcastle United refused to let him go and retained his player registration. Eastham took his employers to the High Court, where he argued that his situation was an unfair restraint of trade. The Court ruled in his favour and this judgement led to the abolition of the 'retain and transfer' system. Eastham was later awarded with an OBE as recognition of his service to football.

BIG IN JAPAN

The first Japanese player to turn out for Arsenal was Junichi Inamoto. The midfielder had been a huge hit at his former club Gamba Osaka, scoring 14 goals in 105 appearances for the Japanese side. He never scored for Arsenal in his handful of first-team appearances but did score with a powerful shot from 30 yards in a reserve match against Chelsea.

MUSICAL GUNNERS

- **Gilberto** plays the mandolin
- **Julio Baptista** strums the ukulele, guitar and banjo
- **Denilson** enjoys playing a Portuguese hand drum
- **Tony Adams** plays the piano
- **Ian Wright** released his own single 'Do The Wright Thing', in 1993

MAGIC NUMBERS: 9 OUT OF 9

- Paul Davis was born on 9 December 1961.

- The number of matches Arsenal played during their victorious FA Cup campaign of 1998.

- The number of Arsenal players left on the pitch as the Gunners battled to a 1–1 draw with PSV Eindhoven in November 2004.

- The number of years Patrick Vieira spent with Arsenal.

- George Armstrong was born on 9 August 1944.

- When Arsenal beat Manchester United in the 2005 FA Cup Final, the teams successfully converted nine spot-kicks between them during the penalty shoot-out.

- Television pundit and former Arsenal striker Alan Smith wore the number 9 shirt during the 1980s and 1990s.

- There were nine goals in the derby dazzler at White Hart Lane in November 2004, when Arsenal beat Tottenham Hotspur 5–4.

- There were nine goals shared between the two teams when Arsenal played Manchester United in the final match played by Matt Busby's Babes in an English stadium in February 1958.

STAND UP POMPEY, POMPEY STOOD UP

Arsenal beat Portsmouth 5–1 at Fratton Park on 6 March 2004. The home fans responded to this demolition by giving Arsenal a standing ovation for the football master-class they had just given their hosts. Arsène Wenger marvelled at this: 'The result is wonderful but it is even more enjoyable to see opposition fans cheering our team.' His opposite number Harry Redknapp agreed: 'I can appreciate great players and it was good to see our fans cheering people like Thierry Henry and Patrick Vieira. They are all athletes, almost monsters. There's no way you can start kicking people like Patrick Vieira. And Henry? He's got to be right up there with the best you have ever seen. When you see his name on the team sheet now as an opposition manager you just say "Oh no".'

DECADE BY DECADE – THE FA CUP

On 5 October 1889, the Club played its first ever FA Cup tie, beating Lyndhurst 11–0. Here is a list of how many games the Club played in the competition in each subsequent decade:

1880s	4
1890s	27
1900s	34
1910s	12
1920s	39
1930s	41
1940s	6
1950s	43
1960s	29
1970s	59
1980s	40
1990s	47

HIGHBURY REMEMBERED (1)

A time capsule containing memories and keepsakes from Arsenal Stadium, Highbury, was placed in Emirates Stadium as a memory of the Club's home for 91 years. The contents of the capsule were:

- A list of every Arsenal player
- A captain's armband once worn by Tony Adams
- A piece of the Highbury turf
- Images of all Arsenal home shirts
- A replica model of Highbury
- A piece of marble, replicating that used in the marble halls at Highbury
- An aerial picture of Highbury
- A stadium flag used at Highbury
- Records of all Arsenal matches ever played at Highbury
- A picture of Ian Wright's celebration after his 'record-breaking' goal
- A history of Arsenal from 1886–present on video
- A history of the Arsenal crest
- A signed shirt from the then first-team squad
- Pictures of all Arsenal managers
- Pictures of all captains in sequence
- A video montage of memorable Arsenal moments
- An image of the clock from the Clock End
- A copy of a newspaper the day the capsule was buried
- A picture of the old North Bank
- Pictures of all the trophies won by Arsenal
- A Highbury match ticket
- An original Arsenal playing shirt worn by David Rocastle
- A guided tour of Highbury on video
- A picture of the 'famous back four'
- Fans' messages
- A signed copy of *Fever Pitch* by Nick Hornby
- A replica home shirt from 1913/14 season, the first season at Highbury
- A photo of Gunnersaurus
- An official Arsenal magazine
- A signed Arsenal Ladies shirt
- Newspaper cuttings documenting the success of the Arsenal Ladies
- A DVD of the 1971 FA Cup Final
- An Emirates Stadium information booklet
- Thierry Henry's socks
- Patrick Vieira's boots
- A matchday programme
- A Club handbook from the unbeaten season of 2003/04
- Images of Emirates Stadium under construction
- A lock of Charlie George's hair

GREAT GOALS (2)

John Jensen
31 December 1994 • Arsenal 1 Queen's Park Rangers 3
Premiership, Highbury

Great goals come at the strangest moments, including in disappointing defeats. John Jensen had signed for Arsenal in the aftermath of his wonder goal in the 1992 European Championship Final. However, his struggles to get on the scoresheet for the Gunners became something of a legend with Arsenal fans shouting 'Shoot!' at the Dane whenever he got the ball. Jensen's moment came in the second half of this game when he received the ball on the edge of the area and curled it home from 30 yards. The strike was received as if it were a World Cup winning goal.

SIXTH TIME LUCKY

When he captained Arsenal to the 1971 FA Cup triumph, Frank McLintock laid a personal ghost to rest. The Scot had reached two FA Cup Finals and one League Cup Final with Leicester City and then played in two League Cup Finals with the Gunners. He was on the losing side for all five of these matches. The 2–1 victory over Liverpool stopped any talk of a jinx.

DID YOU KNOW?

Controversial writer and broadcaster,
David Icke, once had a trial with Arsenal.

KEEPING IT IN THE FAMILY

The first three passes of a football at Emirates Stadium were made between three Dutchmen. Even more incredibly, all three players were from the same family. This is because, for his testimonial match, Dennis Bergkamp had chosen his father Wim to kick off the game. Wim Bergkamp had been battling with cancer and Dennis wanted to mark this by kicking off the game with his father. For good measure, Dennis's son Mitchell joined them in the centre-circle and three generations of the Bergkamp family got football at Emirates Stadium underway.

EUROPE: THE FINAL COUNTDOWN (1)

The 1970 European Fairs Cup

First round

9 September 1969 . . . . **Arsenal 3 Glentoran 0**

29 September 1969 . . . . **Glentoran 1 Arsenal 0**

Second round

20 October 1969 . . . . **Sporting Lisbon 0 Arsenal 0**

26 November 1969 . . . . **Arsenal 3 Sporting Lisbon 0**

Third round

17 December 1970 . . . . **Rouen 0 Arsenal 0**

13 January 1970 . . . . **Arsenal 1 Rouen 0**

Fourth round

11 March 1970 . . . . **Dinamo Bacau 0 Arsenal 2**

18 March 1970 . . . . **Arsenal 7 Dinamo Bacau 1**

Semi-final

8 April 1970 . . . . **Arsenal 3 Ajax 0**

15 April 1970 . . . . **Ajax 1 Arsenal 0**

Final

22 April 1970 . . . . **Anderlecht 1 Arsenal 3**

28 April 1970 . . . . **Arsenal 3 Anderlecht 0**

THE THINGS THEY SAY

'I'm an emotional person and I enjoy crying.
You know the film Beaches *with Bette Midler and Barbara*
Hershey? Sometimes, when I want a good cry, I put it on.'

Ian Wright

A DATE TO REMEMBER (1)

26 April 1986 On the day that an explosion at a nuclear plant caused a disaster in Chernobyl, Arsenal drew 2–2 with West Bromwich Albion.

AKA

A selection of Arsenal nicknames:

Billy McCullough: **Flint**, a character from TV series *Wagon Train*.
Ian McKechnie: **Yuri**, after the first man in space because, following a particularly good performance, his team-mates reckon he was up in the air for days.
Chris Whyte: **Huggy**, a character in US cop series, *Starsky and Hutch*.
Brian Talbot: **Noddy**, the cartoon character.
Perry Groves: **Tintin**, after the comic strip hero.
Kevin Campbell: **Souper Kev**, playing on his surname – a soup brand.
Stefan Schwarz: **Stevie Black**, a literal translation of his name.
Jack Crayston: **Gentleman Jack**.
Thierry Henry: **Titi**.
Abou Diaby: *Le Nettoyeur*, which means 'the cleaner' in French; the name was coined by Henry.

In addition, occasionally Arsenal players have earned a nickname as a group: the midfield trio of David Rocastle, Paul Davis and Michael Thomas were known by some as **The Three Degrees**. The attacking trio of Dennis Bergkamp, Paul Merson and Ian Wright were dubbed **BMW** by one Arsenal fanzine (using the first letter of each of their surnames).

PS: Both Bob Wilson and Steve Williams were nicknamed **Willow** by their Arsenal team-mates.

WHERE ARE THEY NOW? (1)

Between them, the 1989 League Championship winning side produced arguably the most exciting climax to a League campaign ever. But what happened to the Arsenal team from that night?

John Lukic moved back to his first club, Leeds United, and then returned to Arsenal in 1996. He has since coached goalkeepers, including at Arsenal, and most recently with Barnsley.

Lee Dixon co-runs The Riverside Brasserie in Bray, Berkshire and is a BBC football pundit.

David O'Leary now works in the football management field. He has managed Leeds United and Aston Villa.

Steve Bould left Arsenal in 1999 and spent two years with Sunderland AFC. He has now returned to Arsenal, where he coaches the youth team.

Nigel Winterburn spent three years with West Ham United after leaving Arsenal in 2000, and went on to become a television and radio pundit.

David Rocastle, or 'Rocky', joined Leeds United in 1992 and then had spells with Manchester City, Chelsea, Norwich City and Hull City. Sadly, he died in March 2001 at the age of 33.

Kevin Richardson, on leaving Highbury in 1990, enjoyed spells with a number of clubs including Real Sociedad of Spain, Coventry City and Blackpool. He is now a coach at Sunderland AFC.

Michael Thomas moved to Liverpool FC, the team whose hearts he had broken with his famous goal in May 1989. He retired from football in 2001.

Paul Merson signed for Middlesbrough in 1997 and then had playing spells with Aston Villa and Portsmouth among other clubs. He spent three years at Walsall, some of them as coach. He is now a television pundit and a columnist for *The Official Arsenal Magazine*.

Alan Smith, one of the night's goal scorers, went on to score another vital goal for Arsenal – the winner in the 1994 European Cup Winners' Cup Final. He retired owing to injury in 1995 and has since worked as a co-commentator for Sky Sports and as a columnist for the *Daily Telegraph*.

Substitutes
Martin Hayes joined Celtic FC in 1990 and then had spells with Wimbledon, Swansea and Peterborough United before moving to non-league football. He was appointed manager of Bishops Stortford in 1999.

Perry Groves joined Southampton in 1992 but only played 15 games for the Saints before an Achilles tendon injury cut short his career. He now plays for the Arsenal Celebrity XI and works as a sports development manager. His autobiography, *We All Live in a Perry Groves World*, was a surprise success.

RAISING THE CURTAIN

Arsenal have taken part in 19 Charity Shield/Community Shield matches, recognized as the traditional curtain-raiser to the season.

- Arsenal's first one took place on 8 October 1930 against Sheffield Wednesday. Arsenal won 2–1.

- In 1971, despite Arsenal effectively 'qualifying twice' as champions and FA Cup holders, the Club declined to take part in the Charity Shield owing to commitments in European competition. Leicester City, the champions of Division Two, were invited to take Arsenal's place against FA Cup holders, Liverpool. Leicester City won the game 1–0.

- Their meeting with Liverpool on 11 August 1979 was the first time the Gunners played a Charity Shield match at Wembley. Liverpool won the match 3–1.

- Arsenal and Tottenham Hotspur drew 0–0 in the 1991 Charity Shield and consequently shared the trophy for six months each.

- Arsenal were the first winners of the trophy after it was renamed the Community Shield, winning 1–0 against Liverpool on 11 August 2002.

- Their meeting with Liverpool in 2002 was the first time the Gunners played a Charity Shield/Community Shield match at the Millennium Stadium in Cardiff.

SAVING THE BEST FOR FIRST

Pat Jennings made his international debut for Northern Ireland on 15 April 1964. His team beat Wales 3–2. Another debutant for Northern Ireland that day was a young player called George Best.

BORING, BORING ARSENAL (3)

Tony Adams captained Arsenal to League Championships during three different decades. He lifted the trophies in 1989, 1991, 1998 and 2002.

LONG-SERVING GUNNERS

Jack Kelsey made his Arsenal debut in 1951. He played his last match in 1962 and then took over the Club lottery and shop. He subsequently became a commercial manager for the Club until his retirement in 1989. He had been at Highbury for just under four decades.

WHEN DAVE FACED PELÉ

In the 1958 World Cup, the Welsh team put on some great displays and reached the quarter-final. There, they met the mighty Brazil. Arsenal defender Dave Bowen, a key component of the Welsh team, now faced a 17-year-old Pelé. Although the famous Brazilian scored the winner in Brazil's 1–0 victory, Bowen received enormous praise for his performance.

LOCAL PRIDE

Arsenal's 1–1 draw with Tottenham Hotspur on 29 October 2005 was the 150th north London derby. Arsenal's record during the 150 matches was: **Pld 150   W 63   D 38   L 49.**

BERGKAMP AND THE BAGGIES

During Dennis Bergkamp's final season with Arsenal, West Bromwich Albion proved to be significant opponents. The Gunners' visit to the Hawthorns in October 2005 was Dennis Bergkamp's 400th appearance for Arsenal. Then, in the return fixture at Highbury in April 2006, the Dutchman came off the bench to score his 120th, and last, Arsenal goal. The match had been themed as 'Bergkamp Day' and Highbury turned orange in honour of the Dutch master.

THE THINGS THEY SAY

'He's given us unbelievable belief.'

Paul Merson can't believe how great Arsène Wenger is, *1996*

FAMILY FORTUNES

The following Arsenal players had relatives who also plied their trade in the beautiful game:

Vic Groves (1955–64) Uncle of Perry Groves.

Mel Charles (1959–61) Brother of Leeds United and Wales defender John Charles.

George Eastham (1960–66) Son of George Eastham senior, who played for and managed Ards in Northern Ireland.

Dave Bacuzzi (1961–64) Son of Joe Bacuzzi of Fulham.

Trevor Ross (1975–77) Son of Bradford City's William Ross.

John Lukic (1983–90; 1996–2001) Father of John Lukic who played for Nottingham Forest and Grimsby Town.

Andy Linighan (1990–97) Brother of David and Brian Linighan, who played for Ipswich and Sheffield Wednesday respectively.

Ian Wright (1991–98) Stepfather to Shaun Wright-Phillips and father of Southampton's Bradley Wright-Phillips.

Scott Marshall (1992–98) Son of Newcastle goalkeeper Gordon Marshall and brother of Celtic goalkeeper Gordon Marshall (junior).

Christopher Wreh (1997–2000) Cousin of the legendary forward George Weah.

Freddie Ljungberg (1998–) Brother of the Swedish league player Filip Ljungberg.

Nwankwo Kanu (1999–2004) Brother of Chris Kanu, defender for Peterborough United.

Kolo Toure (2002–) Brother of AS Monaco midfielder Yaya Toure.

Justin Hoyte (2003–) Brother of Arsenal youth Gavin Hoyte.

Alexander Hleb (2005–) Brother of footballer Vyacheslav Hleb, midfielder and Belarus international.

NUMBER CRUNCHING (2)

3,038 The total allocation of tickets available for the supporters of clubs visiting Emirates Stadium for Premier League and UEFA Champions League ties. This figure includes tickets for visiting directors and visiting disabled supporters. The figure rises to 9,000 for FA Cup ties.

EMIRATES EXCELLENCE (3)

Emirates Stadium contains enough glass to cover two football pitches.

A RETIRING REF

When Arsenal won the league at White Hart Lane in 1971, it was not just a milestone for the men wearing red and white on the pitch. For the man wearing black it was a big night too. Referee Kevin Howley – a legendary football official, and one of the youngest men ever to take charge of an FA Cup Final – was officiating over his final league match.

DID YOU KNOW?

During the final season at Highbury, 1,044,266 fans came through the turnstiles to watch first-team matches.

ENGLAND EXPECTS

Between them, Tony Adams, Steve Bould, Lee Dixon and Nigel Winterburn formed one of the most celebrated back fours in football history. They won a host of trophies including, between them, 14 League Championships and eight FA Cups. However, on the international stage, their fortunes were mixed.

England caps

Tony Adams	66
Lee Dixon	22
Nigel Winterburn	2
Steve Bould	2

2,000 NOT OUT

The 2,000th match at Highbury came against West Ham United on 1 February 2006. Arsenal's record in these matches is:
Pld 2,000 W 1,189 D 472 L 339 F 4,016 A 1,949.

WORLD CUP 2006

A total of 16 Arsenal players travelled to Germany for the 2006 World Cup Finals. Here is a summary of their fortunes in the tournament:

Jens Lehmann played in all of third-placed Germany's games apart from their third and fourth play-off with Portugal.

Ashley Cole started all five of quarter-finalists England's matches in Germany. **Sol Campbell**, still on Arsenal's books during the tournament, played the final 34 minutes of England's clash with Sweden. **Theo Walcott** was an unused substitute throughout England's World Cup Finals campaign.

Freddie Ljungberg played in four games for Sweden, who reached the second round. He was FIFA's Man Of The Match for the tie against Trinidad and Tobago. He scored Sweden's winner against Paraguay.

Cesc Fabregas played in all four of Spain's games while **Jose Antonio Reyes** played for just 69 minutes of his country's clash with Saudi Arabia. The Spanish reached the second round, where France knocked them out.

Robin van Persie played four games for Holland, who were knocked out by Portugal in the second round.

Thierry Henry reached the Final with France. He was Arsenal's top scorer in the competition with three goals. He was named in the All-star Squad. (The soon-to-be Gunner William Gallas also appeared for France.)

Gilberto played four matches for quarter-finalists Brazil.

Emmanuel Eboue and **Kolo Toure** both made their first World Cup Finals appearances during the competition. Eboue played in all three of his nation's games, Toure in just two. The Ivory Coast finished third in their group and progressed no further.

Philippe Senderos and **Johann Djourou** both played three times for Switzerland. Senderos scored against South Korea. After winning their group, the Swiss exited at the second-round stage.

Tomas Rosicky scored twice against the US and won Man of the Match for that tie. However, the Czechs did not get past the group stage.

Emmanuel Adebayor played in all three of Togo's matches, but the side finished bottom of their group.

2005/06 UEFA CHAMPIONS LEAGUE QUICK FACTS

- Arsenal's first goal in their 2–1 victory away to Ajax in 2005 was the Club's 100th in 70 Champions League games.

- Arsenal became the first English team since Lancashire amateurs, Nelson in 1923, to beat Real Madrid on their own ground. The two-legged tie was the first time that Real Madrid had failed to score in a two-legged Champions League fixture.

- In the first leg against Juventus, Arsenal drew level with AC Milan's record of going seven Champions League matches without conceding. They broke the record in the second leg, when they beat Juventus 2–0.

MAGIC NUMBERS: 8 OUT OF 8

- In his first season with Arsenal, Thierry Henry scored eight goals in European competition.
- Arsenal clinched the 1971 Double on 8 May.
- Goalscoring legend Ian Wright wore the number 8 shirt at Arsenal.
- The length in years of the contract signed by Cesc Fabregas in October 2006. 'Although it looks like a long time, when you think about it at the end of his contract Cesc will be just 27,' said Arsène Wenger.
- The Club's first match after the name was changed from Dial Square to Royal Arsenal was on 8 January 1887.
- Tony Woodcock signed for the Club on 8 June 1982.
- Dennis Bergkamp scored eight goals in total during the 2004/05 season.
- Mike Tiddy scored eight goals for the Club between 1955 and 1958.

TEENAGE KICKS

These Arsenal players were high-achievers even before they turned 20:

Jermaine Pennant
Having already become Notts County's youngest-ever player when he turned out for them at 15 years 341 days, Pennant scored a hat-trick for Arsenal in the 6–1 drubbing of Southampton in 2003. That game was the first of the famous 49-match unbeaten run.

Theo Walcott
The striker is the youngest-ever player to appear in a UEFA Champions League match for Arsenal and the youngest-ever full England international. He is also the youngest-ever player to score for the England under-21s. In 2006, he became the second youngest player ever to score in a League Cup Final.

Cesc Fabregas
He became the Club's youngest player when he appeared against Rotherham United in October 2003, at the age of 16 years and 177 days. In 2005, Cesc won an FA Cup winners' medal at the age of 18. He was also a key part of the team during the latter stages of the 49-match unbeaten run. The Spaniard scored a crucial goal against Juventus during the 2005/06 UEFA Champions League campaign and played in that season's Final. He appeared for Spain in the 2006 World Cup Finals. He played 100 matches for Arsenal before his 20th birthday.

John Radford
The striker became Arsenal's youngest ever hat-trick scorer when he stuck three past Wolverhampton Wanderers in 1965, at the age of 17 years and 315 days.

Ray Kennedy
Having made his first-team Arsenal debut against Glentoran earlier in the competition, Kennedy scored a crucial goal in the first leg of the Fairs Cup Final against Anderlecht in 1970. He was just 18. The following season, while still only 19, Kennedy bagged 26 goals as his team marched to the Double. His most memorable strike of the campaign was the winner in the championship-sealing victory at White Hart Lane.

Paul Vaessen
His headed goal in Arsenal's 1980 European Cup Winners' Cup semi-final inflicted inflicted Juventus's first-ever home defeat by a British side, and sent the Gunners to the Final. He was just 18.

Gael Clichy
The youngest-ever player to win a Premiership medal. He gained the medal at 18 years and 10 months.

Cliff Bastin
Scored 28 goals in 42 games during the title-winning 1930/31 season. He turned 19 during the season.

Nicolas Anelka
Won the Double with Arsenal at the age of 19.

ARSÈNE WENGER: THE FIRST TEN YEARS (2)

First signings
Mr Wenger advised the board to sign Remi Garde and Patrick Vieira. Both joined on 14 August 1996, which meant they arrived at the Club before the new manager did. Remi joined from Strasbourg, Patrick from AC Milan.

First hat-trick
The first hat-trick of the Wenger era came at Filbert Street on August 27 1997 and was delivered by Dennis Bergkamp. All the three goals were breathtaking, and the third was voted Goal of the Season. However, the hat-trick was not enough to gain victory in this tie, which ended 3–3.

EARLY EURO EXITS

Jens Lehmann was red-carded at the Stade de France after just 18 minutes of the 2006 European Cup Final. He was not the first Arsenal goalkeeper to make an untimely exit from such a Final. In 1982, Aston Villa faced Bayern Munich in the European Cup Final at Rotterdam. After just eight minutes, their former Arsenal goalkeeper, Jimmy Rimmer, suffered a shoulder injury that ended his dream night. Aston Villa went on to win the tie 1–0.

THE LATE, LATE SHOW

Any Gunners fans that left these matches early will have missed some moments of drama and significance:

Royal Arsenal 3 Clapton 2 • London Senior Cup semi-final, 28 February 1891

The Gunners were trailing 2–0 with just 25 minutes left of this tie but managed to draw level before Peter Connolly scored the winner in the dying minutes. The Club went on to win the Final against St Bartholomew's Hospital.

Arsenal 2 Hull City 2 • FA Cup semi-final, 22 March 1930

This was an eventful semi-final. Arsenal keeper Dan Lewis was lobbed from 45 yards in the first half and the Gunners eventually found themselves 2–0 behind. Late in the tie, Cliff Bastin received the ball from Alex James and, after a fine run, dispatched it into the top right-hand corner of the goal. The Gunners won the replay and the resultant Final – for the first time ever.

Arsenal 2 Chelsea 2 • FA Cup semi-final, 18 March 1950

The Gunners found themselves 2–1 down against their London rivals when they won a corner late in this tie. Denis Compton urged his brother Leslie to come upfield, but captain Joe Mercer disagreed. Luckily, Leslie followed Denis and headed home his brother's corner to earn Arsenal a replay. The Club went on to beat Liverpool in the Final.

Arsenal 2 Stoke City 2 • FA Cup semi-final, 27 March 1971

On this occasion, Arsenal were trailing 2–1 when referee Pat Partridge added two minutes injury time. Frank McLintock met a corner with his head and Stoke City's John Mahoney handballed on the goal line. Peter Storey's right-footed spot-kick earned Arsenal a replay and sent them on their way to winning the Club's first Double.

Arsenal 2 Southampton 2 • League, 17 September 1988

This is neither a winning goal nor an apparently significant match. However, Alan Smith's late, late equalizer – it came in the seventh minute of injury time – is included because it earned the Gunners a point in a League season that they ultimately won on goals scored. Every point counted during this campaign and all hail Smudger for securing this one! ▸

Sampdoria 3 Arsenal 2 • European Cup Winners' Cup semi-final second leg, 20 April 1995

This is one of those matches for which you need a mathematician! Stefan Schwarz's late free-kick might have seemed a mere consolation goal until it became clear that it took the scores level on aggregate. The game ultimately went to a penalty shoot-out which Arsenal won after Seaman saved three spot-kicks.

Arsenal 2 Bolton Wanderers 1 • Premiership, 5 May 1996

On an exciting final day, the places for the following season's UEFA Cup were decided. Arsenal were losing 1–0 until the closing stages of this game when the previous summer's star signings both scored. First, David Platt equalized and then Dennis Bergkamp scored the winner with a cracking long-range strike. European qualification was assured.

Chelsea 2 Arsenal 2 • Premiership, 6 September 2000

The Gunners have specialized in late goals at Stamford Bridge under Wenger. Nigel Winterburn unleashed a 25-yard late winner there in 1997 and Kanu's spectacular 1999 hat-trick was completed in the closing minutes. Silvinho maintained the tradition here with a long-range equalizer just four minutes from time.

Arsenal 1 Dynamo Kiev 0 • Champions League, 5 November 2003

The Gunners had not won a home tie in the UEFA Champions League for 14 months prior to this match. They looked set to be facing an early exit from the competition until Ashley Cole met Sylvain Wiltord's cross with a diving header to win the match.

PITCH FEVER

Three tonnes of fertilizer were used on the Highbury pitch during the season and 600 litres (130 gallons) of white paint were used to keep the pitch markings nice and fresh. Meanwhile, 800 kg (1,750 lb) of grass seed were used on the pitch throughout the campaign.

CHARITABLE GUNNERS

The Club has done a lot of work for charity, as have many of the men who have pulled on the famous red and white shirt. The following Gunners have all started their own charities:

Bob Wilson: The Willow Foundation
Established in 1999, the charity provides special days out for seriously ill people between the ages of 16 and 40. Among its patrons are former Gunners David Seaman and Pat Jennings.

Nwankwo Kanu: The Kanu Heart Foundation
Kanu nearly lost his life when he was diagnosed with a faulty heart valve. His charity helps African people with heart problems.

Patrick Vieira: The Diambars Academy
The former Arsenal captain set up this school to provide football training for children in Africa. *Diambars* means 'warriors' in Senegal's Wolof language.

Tony Adams: The Sporting Chance Clinic
Formed in September 2000, The Sporting Chance Clinic is a charitable organization dedicated to providing support, counselling, treatment and aftercare to sportsmen and women suffering from addictive illnesses.

The Club has also done a lot of work to support the David Rocastle Trust which was its charity of the season for 2005/06. The David Rocastle Trust primarily supports his family and community projects in his name.

PS: Ian Wright is a patron of the African-Caribbean Leukaemia Trust, while in 2005, David Seaman had his ponytail cut off to raise funds for the Bobby Moore Cancer Research Fund.

EMIRATES EXCELLENCE (4)

Emirates Stadium contains 150 executive boxes, more than three times the number that were at Highbury.

FA BLUES

2001, Arsenal were drawn against Chelsea in the fifth round of the FA up. The Gunners won the tie 3–1 at Highbury. Little did either side know at this would be the first of four consecutive seasons in which the two des would face each other in the competition. In 2002, Arsenal beat helsea 2–0 in the Final, and in 2003 Arsenal beat Chelsea 3–1 in a sixth-und replay at Stamford Bridge. In 2004, the Gunners were once again iumphant as they beat the Blues 2–1 at Highbury in the fifth round. In 05, Chelsea must have been relieved to not face Arsenal again – until ewcastle knocked them out in the fifth round. Meanwhile, the Gunners ent on to win the Final against Manchester United!

FIRST AND LAST

These players all have two 'first names':

Charlie **George**
George **Graham**
Terry **Neill**
Sammy **Nelson**
Pat **Howard**
Charlie **Nicholas**
Michael **Thomas**
Gus **Caesar**
Ryan **Garry**
Thierry **Henry**
Jerome **Thomas**

WENGER INNOVATIONS (3)

hen players are struggling to get over problematic injuries, Wenger is t adverse to sending them overseas for treatment. Both Tony Adams in 97 and Robert Pires in 2002 went to a fitness specialist on the Côte Azure in the South of France and came back all the stronger.

FOLLOW, FOLLOW!

Dennis Bergkamp and Nwankwo Kanu terrified many an opposition defence when they played together at Arsenal. It was a case of 'third time lucky' for the pair, as Arsenal was the third club each had played for though not at the same time until now. Bergkamp was with Ajax between 1986 and 1993, Kanu arrived there in 1993 and left in 1996. Meanwhile the Dutchman was with Inter Milan between 1993 and 1995 and the Nigerian was on their books from 1996 to 1999.

NOT LIKE WATCHING BRAZIL

On 14 April 2001, Arsenal fans witnessed not one, but two, Brazilian Gunners score an own goal in just five minutes of a match against Middlesbrough. First Edu deflected an off-target Middlesbrough shot past David Seaman. Then Silvinho accidentally sent his clearance from a cross into his own net. Of course both players went on to become star players and their misfortune in this tie proved a one-off.

WILD ABOUT THE ROVERS (2)

In the *Roy of the Rovers* cartoon strip, Melchester Rovers' rival clubs were based on real clubs. Therefore, just as Toxteth were based on Liverpool, it is believed that the representation of Arsenal in the strip was the team called Islington. However, some also believe that Melchester Rovers were based on 1950s Arsenal.

LATE STARTERS

Theo Walcott made his professional debut for Southampton at the tender age of 16. However, several players had to wait a lot longer for their first professional game:

> Danny Clapton **20 years old** (Arsenal)
> Bertie Mee **20 years old** (Mansfield Town)
> Ian Wright **21 years old** (Crystal Palace)
> Bob Wilson **22 years old** (Arsenal)

STRANGE INJURIES

...get your dead legs and pulled hamstrings, these are some injuries with a difference:

Alan Skirton Out for 18 months with tuberculosis.
Perry Groves Injured his head bashing it against the dug-out roof while celebrating a goal.
David Seaman Broke a bone reaching for his television remote control.
Steve Morrow Broke his collar bone after falling off Tony Adams's shoulder while celebrating the 1993 League Cup Final victory.
Charlie George Cut off his finger with a lawnmower.
Richard Wright Twisted his ankle while warming up for Everton before a match against Chelsea, having landed on a wooden sign that advised against warming up in that area.
Patrick Vieira After scoring against Manchester United in 1997, the Frenchman injured his knees while celebrating the goal with a slide across the Highbury turf. He didn't return to the team for some weeks.
Thierry Henry When he scored the winning goal in the 2–1 victory over Chelsea in May 2000, he injured himself during the celebrations. The injury appeared to occur when he hit himself in the face with the corner flag in front of the North Bank jumbotron.

LAUREN'S WINS

...2000, Lauren won two international trophies with both finals going to penalty shoot-outs. In February, Cameroon beat Nigeria 4–3 on penalties to lift the African Cup of Nations. Later that year, Cameroon beat Spain, again on penalties, to win the Men's Olympic Football Final.

A FLYING START

...the Arsenal Supporters Club was formed on the eve of the 1949/50 season during a meeting at a cinema on Upper Street in Islington. The members started travelling to away games together and, on Boxing Day 1949, made their first trip by plane to Old Trafford. The 20 supporters who travelled on an old Dakota plane watched their team lose 2–0.

EVANS ABOVE!

In December 1955, Arsenal were cruising 4–0 against Blackpool Highbury. What could possibly go wrong? Left back Dennis Evans recei the ball and, believing he had heard the referee blow the final whis kicked it away in triumph. The ball sailed past his own goalkeeper, (Sullivan. The problem was that the whistle Evans heard had actually co from a member of the crowd. The goal stood and Con Sullivan was den a second successive clean sheet. Arsenal won the game 4–1.

BOB WILSON: A POTTED BIOGRAPHY

Only two men have played a part in all three of Arsenal's Doubles and E Wilson is one of them. Born in Chesterfield on 30 October 1941, the n they call 'Willow' made over 300 appearances for Arsenal and was ev , sent in the 1971 Double team. Although an Englishman who play for the England youth team, Bob Wilson also made two internatio appearances for Scotland.*

His father prevented him taking up an offer with Manchester United a so Wilson instead enrolled at a teacher training college. He then sign for Arsenal and made his Gunners' debut in 1963 as an amateur – the l amateur to play in the English top flight. However, he had to wait f years to become first-choice goalkeeper for Arsenal.

He retired as a player at the age of 32 in 1974 and immediately turned broadcasting. He established himself as a household name for his we on BBC and then iTV. He was also featured in a comic strip when signed for the fictional Melchester Rovers side in the *Roy of the Rov* series. He returned to Arsenal as a coach, training the likes of I Jennings and David Seaman.

After a long fight with breast cancer, Wilson's daughter, Anna, died 1998. The following year, Wilson set up The Willow Foundation, a char to help those with life-threatening illnesses.

* Midfielder Trevor Ross had a similar experience: he played for the England Schoolboy Team and went on to appear for the Scotland under-21s.

DID YOU KNOW?

The Premiership's 15,000th goal was scored by former Gunner Moriz Volz for Fulham against Chelsea on 30 December 2006.

THE THINGS THEY SAY

'I am a thunderstorm protector.'

Arsène Wenger promises to defend his players
from media criticism, *August 1997*

HE'S ALL RIGHT, JACK

It was hardly the most auspicious start for any football career. Jack Kelsey conceded five goals in his Arsenal debut against Charlton Athletic on 24 February 1951. A local music-hall comedian turned on Kelsey in his act. However, manager Tom Whittaker defended his goalkeeper and compared him to an unlucky pilot, shot down on his first mission. Whittaker was proved right when Kelsey went on to win the League Championship in 1953 and amass some 41 international caps for Wales.

DUTCH MASTER

Robin van Persie is a very creative player on the pitch and his father Bob has a different creative strength: he is a respected artist in Holland. However, his art still has a football dimension. As Robin explains:

'He got his inspiration years ago from looking at all the people at the other end of a football stadium and not being able to see the detail in their faces, just the shape. He makes models of people from balls of paper and magazines. They are like statues and they are all different, just like people are all different shapes and sizes. My Dad is an artistic kind of guy, he can look at the countryside and see beauty in the shapes of the bushes and trees.'

A COLLECTION OF CURIOUS CAMPAIGNS

- During the 1899/1900 season, Arsenal conceded 43 goals. In season 1999/2000, Arsenal also conceded 43 goals.

- Only three fixtures of the 1939/40 season had been completed when the Second World War broke out. The season was then abandoned.

- Arsenal played the final match of the 1946/47 season on 7 June 1947. A particularly cold winter had resulted in multiple match postponements during the winter months. The following campaign kicked off just 11 weeks later, on 23 August.

- The Gunners finished the 1948/49 season on 49 points and amassed the same number of points in the 1949/50 season.

- In the 1973/74 season, Arsenal won 14 matches, lost 14 matches and drew 14 matches.

- The most games Arsenal have played in one season stands at 70. This happened in the 1979/80 season. The total is made up of 42 League matches, 11 FA Cup matches, nine Cup Winners' Cup ties, seven League Cup ties and one Charity Shield match. Arsenal won 30, lost 11 and drew 29 of these matches.

- For the 1991/92 season, Arsenal were the top scorers over all the competitions, netting – appropriately enough – 92 goals.

- For the 1992/93 season, the Gunners went from the League's top scorers to the League's lowest scorers. They did, however, boast the Premiership's second best defence.

ISLINGTON UNCOVERED (3)

It is believed that there was once a Roman garrison situated at the top of Highbury Hill. This has never been completely proven, but streets off Highbury Place are named after Roman colonies: Calabria and Baalbec.

THE CENTURIONS

Players who have scored 100 or more goals for Arsenal:

1 Thierry Henry **226**
2 Ian Wright **185**
3 Cliff Bastin **178**
4 John Radford **149**
5 Jimmy Brain **139**
5= Ted Drake **139**
7 Doug Lishman **137**
8 Joe Hulme **125**
9 David Jack **124**
10 Dennis Bergkamp **120**
11 Reg Lewis **118**
12 Alan Smith **115**
13 Jack Lambert **109**
14 Frank Stapleton **108**
15 David Herd **107**
16 Joe Baker **100**

WHAT'S IN A NAME? (1)

He might have a slightly unusual name, but former Arsenal winger Perry Groves could have had an even more tittersome title, as he recalls:

'My folks were big fans of the actor Pernell Roberts who played Adam in the popular cowboy series Bonanza *on TV. They actually toyed with the idea of calling me Pernell for a while. "Pernell Groves" – the very sound of it gives me a chill!'*

From *We All Live in a Perry Groves World* by Perry Groves

PS: Joe Haverty, who played for Arsenal from 1954–61 was nicknamed Little Joe, also after a character in *Bonanza*.

ABOUT THE CENTURIONS

- Joe Baker is one of only two players to have made his international debut for England having never played in the English League.

- Jack Lambert was killed in a car accident in 1940. In 1962, Joe Baker was lucky to survive a serious car accident, as was his passenger, Denis Law.

- Alan Smith received only one booking in his entire career – it came in the 1993 FA Cup Final replay against Sheffield Wednesday.

- David Jack's full name was David Bone Nightingale Jack. He scored the first goal at Wembley Stadium for Bolton Wanderers during the 1923 FA Cup Final.

- Joe Hulme worked as a policeman during the Second World War.

- Doug Lishman worked for the Boots chemist chain after retirement.

THE THINGS THEY SAY

It's okay, I didn't really want him, he's not good enough for us anyway.'

Bill Shankly pretends he isn't disappointed when Bob McNab joins Arsenal, turning down the chance to sign for Liverpool

JOE MERCER'S CONCUSSION

When Arsenal beat Stoke City 3–0 at Highbury on 20 September 1947, Joe Mercer approached team-mate Jimmy Logie a few minutes before the end of the game to ask: 'What's the score?' Why did Mercer not know what the score was? An injury he had picked up had given him mild concussion. However, he had been playing so well that nobody had suspected for a moment.

ISLINGTON UNCOVERED (4)

The Highbury Barn pub is a popular meeting place for Arsenal supporters to gather on matchday. Originally called The Barn Tea and Pleasure Gardens, in 1870 the venue played host to a group of French dancers who caused such outrage with their routine that the venue was forced to close!

THE THINGS THEY SAY

'When I stood up to do the speech my shirt was soaking with sweat. It was a fantastic experience though. I told the groom that it was like when I played against Chelsea for Arsenal for the first time. I was under pressure to do well.'

Gael Clichy on his best-man duties at a friend's wedding

WE LUVVIE YOU ARSENAL!

During 1998, Emmanuel Petit won the Double with Arsenal and scored the crowning goal in France's World Cup Final victory over Brazil. As if that wasn't enough, Petit also starred in a Christmas special edition of ITV's popular long-running police drama *The Bill*. Other instances of acting Arsenal aces include:

Sol Campbell in *Footballers' Wives*
David Seaman in *Brookside*
Luis Boa Morte in *Grange Hill*

TERRIFIC THIERRY (2)

Thierry Henry is France's leading scorer in the three World Cup Finals in which he has taken part. He scored three in the 1998 campaign, none in 2002 (no French player scored that summer) and three in 2006.

JOIN OUR CLUB

To qualify to become an official Arsenal Supporters Club, a club must:

- Consist of at least 30 members.

- Be set up beyond a 48-km (30-mile) radius of all other Arsenal Supporters Clubs.

- Form a committee comprising Chairperson, Secretary, Treasurer.

- Submit two personal references for these members from an employer or professional person of some standing in the community.

- Hold at least three committee meetings per season and an Annual General Meeting to which all members must be invited.

- Have access to a minimum of one computer with internet and email.

MAGIC NUMBERS: 7 OUT OF 7

- Ronnie Rooke, top scorer in Arsenal's 1948 League Championship season, was born on 7 December 1911.

- Paolo Vernazza made just seven appearances for Arsenal during his career at the Club, which began in 1997 and ended in 2000.

- Kolo Toure scored seven goals in his first 200 games for Arsenal.

- David Platt wore the number 7 shirt. He announced his retirement on 7 July 1998.

- Arsenal legends who have worn the number 7 shirt include Liam Brady, David Rocastle and Robert Pires.

- Jose Antonio Reyes started seven League games during the 2003/04 season (out of a total of 13 appearances).

- Jermaine Pennant's only goals for Arsenal were a hat-trick against Southampton on 7 May 2003.

THOMAS BROWN MITCHELL 1897–98

Pld	W	D	L	F	A	Pts
30	16	5	9	69	37	37

GEORGE ELCOAT 1898–99

Pld	W	D	L	F	A	Pts
34	18	5	11	72	41	41

HARRY BRADSHAW 1899–1904

Pld	W	D	L	F	A	Pts
170	90	31	49	307	156	211

PHIL KELSO 1904–08

Pld	W	D	L	F	A	Pts
148	59	32	57	215	226	150

GEORGE MORRELL 1908–15

Pld	W	D	L	F	A	Pts
266	95	65	106	334	377	255

LESLIE KNIGHTON 1919–25

Pld	W	D	L	F	A	Pts
252	87	57	108	309	360	231

HERBERT CHAPMAN 1925–34

Pld	W	D	L	F	A	Pts
359	171	90	98	777	561	432

GEORGE ALLISON 1934–47

Pld	W	D	L	F	A	Pts
271	123	74	74	511	325	320

TOM WHITTAKER 1947–56

Pld	W	D	L	F	A	Pts
392	178	102	112	719	534	458

JACK CRAYSTON 1956–58

Pld	W	D	L	F	A	Pts
70	30	14	26	127	129	89

GEORGE SWINDIN 1958–62

Pld	W	D	L	F	A	Pts
168	67	39	62	304	305	173

BILLY WRIGHT 1962–66

Pld	W	D	L	F	A	Pts
168	64	41	63	307	309	169

BERTIE MEE 1966–76

Pld	W	D	L	F	A	Pts
420	181	115	124	554	444	477

TERRY NEILL 1976–83

Pld	W	D	L	F	A	Pts
311	134	87	90	431	343	398

DON HOWE 1984–86

Pld	W	D	L	F	A	Pts
98	47	25	26	150	116	166

GEORGE GRAHAM 1986–95

Pld	W	D	L	F	A	Pts
350	162	106	82	522	310	592

STEWART HOUSTON 1995 AND 1996

Pld	W	D	L	F	A	Pts
14	5	2	7	21	17	17

BRUCE RIOCH 1995–96

Pld	W	D	L	F	A	Pts
38	17	12	9	49	32	63

ARSÈNE WENGER 1996–

Pld	W	D	L	F	A	Pts
411	241	100	70	772	361	826

There are no official records of Sam Hollis's statistics.

EUROPE: THE FINAL COUNTDOWN (2)
The 1980 European Cup Winners' Cup

First round

19 September 1979 . . . . **Arsenal 2 Fenerbahçe 0**

3 October 1979 . . . . **Fenerbahçe 0 Arsenal 0**

Second round

24 October 1979 . . . . **Arsenal 2 Magdeburg 1**

7 November 1979 . . . . **Magdeburg 2 Arsenal 2**

Quarter-final

5 March 1980 . . . . **Arsenal 5 IFK Gothenburg 1**

19 March 1980 . . . . **IFK Gothenburg 0 Arsenal 0**

Semi-final

9 April 1980 . . . . **Arsenal 1 Juventus 1**

23 April 1980 . . . . **Juventus 0 Arsenal 1**

Final

14 May 1980 . . . . **Arsenal 0 Valencia 0**

(Arsenal lost 4–5 on penalties)

GREAT GOALS (3)

Anders Limpar
20 April 1992 • Arsenal 4 Liverpool 0
First Division, Highbury

The Gunners went goal crazy during the run-in of the 1991/92 season and this goal was the best of the lot. Picking up the ball 50 yards from goal, super-Swede Anders Limpar unleashed a perfect lob that beat Mike Hooper and sailed into the back of the net.

GETTING SHIRTY

David Platt signed for Arsenal in 1995 and left three years later having been a key part of a Double-winning side. However, this was not the first time 'Platty' had played at Highbury in an Arsenal shirt.

Arsenal hosted Aston Villa at Highbury on 3 April 1991. The home side were 4–0 ahead when the visiting goalkeeper Nigel Spink injured his arm and was forced to leave the field. Platt was nominated as an emergency replacement in goal but as a safety precaution owing to the injury, Spink was not allowed to remove his shirt and give it to Platt.

Therefore, Platt was forced to don a spare Arsenal goalkeeper's shirt, which he did as the home fans sang 'You'll never play for Arsenal!' Platt performed well in goal and only conceded one further goal – from Kevin Campbell.

This was not the first time an outfield player had been forced to don an Arsenal shirt and go between the sticks. During a match at Leicester in August 1963, Arsenal goalkeeper Jack McClelland was injured. Arsenal striker Joe Baker rose to the challenge and went in goal. He conceded five goals but won respect for his bravery and efforts.

WHAT'S IN A NAME? (2)

Dennis Bergkamp was named after Manchester United legend Denis Law. Dennis's parents just added an extra 'n' to his name.

CAPITAL VENTURES

Former Arsenal captain, Thierry Henry, might have been born in Paris in 1977, but the French capital has not always been the kindest city to Arsenal folk.

Arsenal's annual tie with Racing Club of Paris was a long-held tradition. However, one year, it nearly caused a disaster. In November 1938, two aeroplanes took off from the UK to fly the Arsenal team to Paris for the tie. However, thick fog covered the French capital. The first plane landed safely but the second one had to abort landing at the last moment and nearly crashed into a aircraft hangar. It eventually landed safely. The team drew the match 1–1.

The 1995 European Cup Winners' Cup Final held in Paris was a bitter experience for all Arsenal fans. With the sides at 1–1, a penalty shoot-out seemed likely and, given David Seaman's fine record at spot-kicks, Gunners fans could be confident of victory. However, in the final minutes former Spurs midfielder Nayim lobbed Seaman from the halfway line and robbed Arsenal of a second successive European Cup Winners' Cup.

The 2006 UEFA Champions League Final was another evening of heartbreak in Paris for the Gunners. Reduced to ten men after the dismissal of Jens Lehmann, the Gunners took the lead through Sol Campbell in the 37th minute. However, during the final 14 minutes the Spanish giants struck twice to win the trophy.

MYSTIC MAN

When Arsenal won the 1950 FA Cup Final at Wembley, it brought joy to everyone associated with the Club. The team had gone through a difficult period earlier in the campaign and many felt that a number of players were past their peak.

However, for one Arsenal player the result was no surprise at all. Four months before the Final, goalkeeper George Swindin had told team-mate Joe Mercer that Arsenal would be drawn at home four times in the FA Cup and win the trophy. Sure enough, Arsenal enjoyed a run of home ties and went on to win the FA Cup, beating Liverpool 2–0 in the Final!

A TOP TEN

Have you ever wondered what was Number One in the charts the day that your favourite Arsenal player was born?

Liam Brady *13 February 1956*
'Memories are Made of This', Dean Martin
Charlie Nicholas *30 December 1961*
'Moon River', Danny Williams,
Ian Wright *3 November 1963*
'You'll Never Walk Alone', Gerry and the Pacemakers
Tony Adams *10 October 1966*
'Distant Drums', Jim Reeves
Jens Lehmann *10 November 1969*
'Sugar Sugar', The Archies
Robert Pires *29 October 1973*
'Daydreamer/The Puppy Song', David Cassidy
Freddie Ljungberg *16 April 1977*
'Knowing Me, Knowing You', ABBA
Robin van Persie *6 August 1983*
'Wherever I Lay My Hat (That's My Home)', Paul Young
Cesc Fabregas *4 May 1987*
'Nothing's Gonna Stop Us Now', Starship
Theo Walcott *16 March 1989*
'Too Many Broken Hearts', Jason Donovan

DID YOU KNOW?

When Arsenal won the title at Anfield in 1989, Theo Walcott was just 2 months and 10 days old.

EMIRATES EXCELLENCE (5)

Fresh air can be blown onto the pitch, supplying additional oxygen to the area around the grass roots, which helps provide a more healthy playing surface. Excess water is drawn off by a vacuum system.

TOAST OF THE TOWN

The following is taken from a report in the *Kentish Independent* of the scenes in Plumstead that followed Arsenal's 6–0 victory over St Bartholomew's Hospital in the Final of the 1891 London Senior Cup:

> *'There were celebrations everywhere all evening and, we fear, a good deal of drinking was mixed with the rejoicing and exultation.'*

JACK HUMBLE: A POTTED BIOGRAPHY

Born in the Durham village of East Hartburn in 1862, Jack Humble was one of the founding fathers of Arsenal and a hugely important figure in the history of the Club. Humble's mother and father died within months of each other while he was a teenager. He and his elder brother decided to leave the impoverished northeast for London. They couldn't afford the train fare so they walked the entire 640-km (400-mile) trip.

Once they arrived in the capital, the Humble brothers found work as engine fitters at the Royal Arsenal. A left-wing man, Humble defended the rights of workers and campaigned for more leisure time for his colleagues and himself. During that time, he helped found Dial Square and then Royal Arsenal.

In 1891, Humble realized that it was easy for professional clubs to tempt Arsenal players away so he proposed that the Club turn professional. However, when it was proposed that the Club become a limited company, Humble said: 'The Club has been founded by working men and it is my ambition to see it carried on by them.' Humble's proposition that the Club turn professional was acted on two years later, while his objections to the Club becoming a limited company were overlooked.

Nevertheless, Humble remained a director of the Club for some years. During this time, he also became the Club's de facto historian. In 1929, the FA made him resign as a result of a scandal at the Club. Although he was entirely innocent he was forced to leave because the FA deemed that he should have prevented the scandal. He died on an uncertain date during the 1930s but not before he had witnessed the beginning of Herbert Chapman's glorious reign.

KITTED OUT

Vic Akers is the Arsenal Kit Manager and the Arsenal Ladies Manager. Here he describes a typical matchday in the life of a Kit Manager:

'Paul [Akers, Assistant Kit Manager] and I will get into the stadium at around 10 am for a 3 pm kick-off. Having dropped the kit off the night before we'll finish setting up. The opposition kit men will arrive and it will be our job to liaise with them and show them around the new facilities at Emirates Stadium.

'During a match I'll sit in the dug out. Footwear is often an issue, with studs coming loose, and so you have to be aware of this and be prepared for everything. Once, for example, up at Birmingham, the sole of one of Kolo Toure's boots actually came off!

'We'll have stuff ready in the dressing room for such matters and we have to be quick off the mark to get that to the players as soon as possible. It's a question of reacting quickly and finding a solution when and where we can.

'After a match, Paul and I are often the last ones to leave the dressing room. That'll be about an hour and a half after the players have left. We then get everything together and pack it away to be washed.

'My nightmare is not having the right kit for a player. We once had to send for a pair of boots for a player who was called up late to the squad. They were sent up on the supporters' coach so that was a lucky escape!'

HARD-HEADED

Morris Bates was also known as 'The Iron-Headed Man' because he was regularly willing to head the heavy, solid footballs that were in use when he was playing, in the 1880s.

DOH!

Shortly after taking over at Arsenal, George Allison was giving a team talk to his side in preparation for the following day's match. He warned them at some length about Charlie Napier, the Sheffield Wednesday player, who he predicted would be the major danger facing them. One of the team, Jack Crayston, tried to interrupt but Allison insisted that he be allowed to finish. Only when he finished was Crayston able to tell his manager that while he agreed Napier was Sheffield Wednesday's key player, Arsenal were actually playing Blackpool the following day.

A COTTAGE INDUSTRY

Nine of the first 14 managers of Fulham FC had either played for or managed Arsenal. This number includes Phil Kelso who managed Arsenal, resigned to run a hotel in Scotland but then quickly replaced Harry Bradshaw as Fulham manager.

THORPE PARKED

It has been said that a penalty shoot-out is an unfair way to settle an FA Cup tie, but during Arsenal's first campaign in the FA Cup, in 1889/90, there was a much more unfair reason for victory. After beating Lyndhurst 11–0 in their opening tie, Arsenal were drawn away to Thorpe. The sides drew 2–2 but Arsenal went through because Thorpe could not afford to travel to London for a replay.

PUSKAS WAS A GUNNER!

Ferenc Puskas was one of football's finest ever players. Between the 1940s and 1960s he starred for clubs including Real Madrid and for the Hungarian national side. And he was an Arsenal fan! As a youngster, Puskas read about Herbert Chapman's accomplishments at Highbury in the Hungarian press. As you no doubt know from the first *Arsenal Miscellany*, he once said: 'There was only one side for me – Arsenal.' He was even photographed in an Arsenal shirt once, playing keepy-uppy alongside England goalkeeper Gordon Banks.

A WONDERFUL YEAR

Dial Square FC, which later became Arsenal FC, was formed in 1886. Here are ten other noteworthy events that year:

1 England's Hockey Association was formed.
2 The first train-load of oranges was transported out of Los Angeles via an intercontinental railroad.
3 The first adverts for Coca-Cola appeared.
4 Britain annexed Burma.
5 A hurricane demolished Indianola in Texas.
6 London's Shaftesbury Avenue was completed.
7 The General Strike began in the United States.
8 The Statue of Liberty dedication ceremony took place.
9 The South African city of Johannesburg was established.
10 Clarence Birdseye, godfather of the frozen food industry, was born.

MAGIC NUMBERS: 6 OUT OF 6

- Jimmy Carter left Arsenal for Portsmouth on 6 July 1995. He had appeared 29 times for Arsenal and scored two goals for the Club.

- Arsenal scored six goals in their opening two home matches of the 1914/15 season. They beat Glossop North End 3–0 and then beat Fulham by the same margin 11 days later.

- Vic Groves scored six goals in the FA Cup for Arsenal between 1955 and 1963.

- Stewart Robson, Arsenal Player of the Year in 1985, was born on 6 November 1964.

- Jay Simpson scored six goals in the Barclays Premiership Reserve League South in 2005/06.

- Brian Talbot spent six years with the Club between 1979 and 1985. He made 327 appearances and scored 49 goals.

BORING, BORING ARSENAL (4)

On 12 March 1900, Arsenal beat Loughborough 12–0.

SHORT AND SWEET (1)

Bruce Rioch was in charge at Arsenal for just 61 weeks – the shortest term for any Arsenal manager. In that time he signed Dennis Bergkamp and David Platt, took the Gunners to the semi-finals of the League Cup and secured UEFA Cup football for the following season.

MURAL

In 1992, as work was in progress constructing the new North Bank at Highbury, a huge mural was erected in front of the emerging stand. The mural was 68.5 metres (75 yards) long, 16.5 metres (18 yards) high and covered in total an area of over 1,000 square metres (12,000 square feet).

The mural depicted an Arsenal crowd but it had to be repainted after an oversight was pointed out. All the faces in the crowd were white, so it was repainted to reflect the ethnic diversity of the Highbury crowd.

For the first match played in front of the mural, a skydiver parachuted into the stadium. He was supposed to land in the centre-circle but missed his intended landing spot and instead disappeared behind the mural.

Dubbed 'Muriel' by some, the mural was believed, for a while, to have a curse on the team's scoring efforts. It was only during the sixth match played in front of the mural – a 1–0 victory over Manchester City – that Arsenal scored at the North End of the ground, where the mural was located.

FIVE STAR

When Herbert Chapman was appointed Arsenal manager in 1925, he predicted that it would take him five years to build a winning team. Five years to the week later, his team proved him right when they landed the FA Cup, the first major trophy of his reign and the Club's history.

WHAT IAN DID NEXT

Ian Wright left Arsenal in 1998 and enjoyed spells with West Ham United, Nottingham Forest, Celtic and Burnley before retiring in 2000. Since he has retired from football, it has been all-go for Wrighty, who has:

2000 Received an MBE for services to football.

2001– Appeared as a pundit on BBC's *Match Of The Day* for domestic and international matches. This was followed by subsequent television and radio appearances including *The National Lottery, Friends Like These, Wright & Bright, Guinness World Records, What Kids Really Think, They Think It's All Over, Top Gear, Wright Across America, Friday Night Project* and *Ian Wright's Unfit Kids*.

2005 Been inducted into the English Football Hall of Fame.

2006 Backed tourism in Israel when he gave a speech at a party at Emirates Stadium thrown by the Israeli Government Tourist Office.

Spoken out against homophobia in football: 'When people go into an office they don't have to be subjected to discrimination whether they are homosexual, fat, black, thin, tall, small. It's not going to happen to somebody in an office so why should it happen on the pitch?'

DUTCH COURAGE

No wonder the likes of Marc Overmars, Dennis Bergkamp and Robin van Persie felt so at home at Arsenal – the grass seeds used at Highbury were perennial rye grass seeds from Holland.

PROGRAMME NOTES

'This blooding of youngsters is a ticklish business. However promising a man may look in the reserves, you cannot know whether he will survive the extra speed, cleverer positioning and the tense atmosphere of the senior side … The grooming of an Arsenal youngster takes a matter of years.'

Bernard Joy, Arsenal programme, *April 1951*

KEEPING UP WITH JONES

When Bryn Jones signed for Arsenal in 1938, the fee was £14,000 which was the record fee in English football. Being the most expensive player in English football proved a heavy burden for Jones to shoulder.

Although he started well at Arsenal, Jones still felt that the weight of expectation on him was difficult to cope with. He and his manager agreed that a spell in the reserves would be beneficial as it would take some of the attention off him. However, a massive 33,000 people turned up to watch his first match in the reserves so the venture proved anything but successful in removing Jones from the limelight.

Of course, subsequent transfers broke the record Jones had set and other players became the most expensive ever. These included Jones's nephew Cliff who became the then most expensive player when he signed for Spurs for £35,000 in the 1950s.

BLOOD AND GUTS

During Arsenal's glorious march to FA Cup victory in the 1992/93 season, on two occasions centre backs nodded home a goal against physical odds. In the sixth-round match against Ipswich Town at Portman Road, captain Tony Adams rose to head Arsenal's first goal despite the fact that he had stitches in his head. During the Final against Sheffield Wednesday, his defensive partner Andy Linighan headed home the winner despite having a broken nose from an earlier clash with Owls striker Mark Bright. When asked at the end of the match how his nose was, Linighan shrugged: 'I don't think I'll be picking it for a while.'

However, both of these moments of bravery are eclipsed by Ted Drake's courage during a match in the 1937/38 season. The match was against Brentford at Griffin Park on 18 April. Drake was knocked out, but insisted on returning to the field with blood pouring down his face from a severe head wound. He ended the game half-conscious and slung over the shoulders of Tom Whittaker. He had suffered two broken bones in one wrist and needed nine stitches in his head wound.

THE ITALIAN JOB

When Arsenal beat Inter Milan 5–1 at the San Siro Stadium in 2003, they became the first British team to beat the Italian giants on their own turf since Birmingham City in the 1960/61 season.

WORTH THE PAPER IT IS WRITTEN ON

Extracts from the contract drawn up between the Club and Billy Wright when he was appointed Manager on 7 September 1962:

'The Manager shall at all times during the continuance of this Agreement have and exercise all powers and discretions and perform do and carry out all duties acts matters and things as directed by the Board of Directors of the Club and in particular shall:

'a) Superintend direct and have control over the coaches and trainers and the players engaged by the Club

'b) Generally superintend the training coaching employment welfare and recreation of the players engaged by the Club

'c) Select all teams for matches in which the Club shall be engaged

'd) Superintend recruitment of new players

'In consideration for the services to be rendered by the Manager, the Club hereby agrees with the Manager to pay him a salary at the rate of £3,000 per annum together with a further sum at the rate of £500 per annum as a contribution towards his extraneous expenses making a totality of £3,500 per annum. The said sums shall be payable by thirteen equal instalments on every fourth Saturday.'

FASHIONABLE GUNNERS (1)

Arsenal players have always had a lot of style on and off the pitch:

- Together with Terry Venables and Ron Harris, George Graham opened a tailoring business known as **Grateron** – which is a combination of abbreviated versions of their names.

- Emmanuel Petit opened a clothing store in London's Sloane Street with French designer **Jitrois**.

- Former Gunner Robert Pires modelled for **French Connection**.

- Another former Arsenal star, Thierry Henry, is an international ambassador for **Tommy Hilfiger**.

- Freddie Ljungberg has famously modelled underwear for **Calvin Klein**.

LET THERE BE LIGHT

In 1959, Colchester United, then of the Third Division, were drawn against First Division leaders Arsenal in the fourth round of the FA Cup. After gaining a creditable 2–2 draw in front of 16,000 fans at Layer Road, Colchester United were beaten 4–0 in the replay at Highbury. However, nobody went home from the tie empty-handed. The money Colchester United received from the two matches helped to pay for the first floodlights at Layer Road.

DOUBLE OR QUITS

The 1934/35 season saw Arsenal finish the campaign with nearly twice the number of points of north London rivals Tottenham Hotspur. The Gunners won the title with 58 points, while Tottenham finished bottom of the league with 30 points.

WHEN ARSENAL WON THE TREBLE ...

Arsenal's 2–1 victory over Liverpool in the 1971 FA Cup Final secured the Club's first Double. However, the Club won a third trophy that season when they beat Cardiff City 2–0 on aggregate in the Final of the FA Youth Cup. The trophy was proudly displayed on the open-top bus parade from Highbury to Islington Town Hall.

This 'Treble' was celebrated by the FA with a certificate donated to the Club. It read 'This treble success has never previously been achieved during the history of The Football Association and the Council wishes to mark the event by extending the heartiest congratulations to the officials and players responsible for this meritorious performance.'

WAR BABY (1)

The fortunes of Arsenal and the local area during the Second World War:

- In October 1940, a bomb weighing 450 kg (1,000 lb) fell near the Arsenal stadium. Several RAF men were sitting in a hut that was blown up. Two of them died. Tonnes of concrete were blown over the Clock End terraces.

- On 16 April 1941, five bombs fell through the North Bank roof. Fire broke out and the roof collapsed. The goalposts in front of the North Bank were destroyed by the fire.

- During the hostilities, Islington residents took shelter in the Arsenal Underground station.

EXCEPTIONAL RULES

The *Players Instructions and Training Rules* book was compiled in the 1940s by Assistant Manager Jack Crayston and approved by Manager Tom Whittaker. It had to be produced to the Commissionaire at the official entrance to Highbury to gain access to the stadium.

The rules included:

'All players who are not engaged in business shall attend the grounds for training punctually at 10 am, daily (matchdays excepted) and shall be under the orders of the trainers for the remainder of the day. All players engaged in business during the day must attend at the grounds for training on Tuesday and Thursday evenings (or oftener if required) between 6 and 8 pm, unless they have made other arrangements for training that have been approved by the manager.

'All players who have not been selected to play in any of the teams, and who have not been advised otherwise must be at the ground on matchdays and report to the trainer in time to strip and play should any emergency arise and their pre-match meal must be adjusted accordingly.

'Immediately players receive information that they are selected to play in a match, they must see their playing kit is in proper condition, and particular attention must be given to the boots which must be in accordance with FA regulations.

'There has been cause for complaint of the excessive use of stores belonging to the Club, particularly medicine, and it has recently developed into abuse. Players will use all stores with the greatest economy.

'No smoking will be permitted in the dressing rooms. Players selected in matches, and reserves, must refrain from smoking after 11 am on the matchday until the match is over.

'The player shall not engage in any business or live in any place which the directors (or committee) of the Club deem undesirable.

'Members of the Arsenal staff are available at all times to assist you in any playing or domestic problems you may have. Do not hesitate to call upon them.'

SITUATIONS VACANT

'Arsenal Football Club is open to receive applications for the position of Team Manager. He must be experienced and possess the highest qualifications for the post, both as to ability and personal character. Gentlemen whose sole ability to build up a good side depends on the payment of heavy and exorbitant transfer fees need not apply.'

Advertisement for the vacant manager's position in the *Athletic News*, *1925*. The spot was filled by Herbert Chapman.

SELF-FELICITATION

'A year ago we were congratulating ourselves on having brought to Highbury the world-famed FA Challenge Cup. Today we have even greater grounds for self-felicitation. The League Championship Cup admittedly does not carry with it the glamour which enshrouds the trophy which was ours twelve months ago, but nevertheless it is beyond doubt an emblem of greater merit than that represented by the famous Cup.

'So in our elation it is perhaps pardonable that we should be a little self-centred and I am sure that Bolton Wanderers, who know themselves what a moment of triumph means (for they alone of all clubs have won the FA Cup three times at Wembley) will excuse us if we postpone our welcome to them while we dilate on the League tournament which closes today.'

Programme notes for Arsenal v Bolton, *2 May 1931*

ROYAL APPOINTMENT

Over the years, many members of the Royal Family have visited Highbury:

4 February 1922: **HRH The Duke of York** attended a
League match against Newcastle United.
5 April 1930: **Prince George** attended an inter-service match
between the Army, the Royal Navy and the Royal Marines.
1 December 1932: **HRH Prince of Wales** opened the
West Stand and watched a League clash with Chelsea.
12 May 1934: **HRH The Duke Of York** attended a schoolboy
international between England and Scotland.
14 November 1934: **HRH Prince Arthur of Connaught**
watched the England v Italy match.
20 April 1936: **HRH The Duke of Kent** attended
the Civil Service XI v Durham.
22 October 1952: **HRH The Duke of Edinburgh** watched
a charity match between Arsenal and Hibernian.
16 November 1965: **HRH The Duke of Edinburgh**
attended Arsenal v Brazil XI.
15 February 1994: **HRH The Duke of Kent**
opened the new North Bank stand.
2 February 2000: **HRH The Duke of Edinburgh**
attended an Arsenal Double Club event.
15 December 2003: **HRH The Prince of Wales**
attended a Prince's Trust event in the South Stand.
26 October 2006: **HRH The Duke of Edinburgh** opened
Emirates Stadium.

Occasionally, royalty from other countries also visit the Club. On 23 June 2005, King Osagyefo Oseadeeyo Agyemang Badu II of the Dormaa Traditional Area in Ghana was shown around Highbury. He brought with him greetings from the management and players of Berekum Arsenal FC who are from his kingdom.

BORING, BORING ARSENAL (5)

The Gunners scored 127 League goals during the 1930/31 season.

ABSORBING THE GREEK

Stathis Tavlaridis is the only Greek to have played for Arsenal. The defender left the Club in 2004 having made seven first-team starts and one substitute appearance. However, there is one Greek who has remained part of the Club. Fred the Greek is a statue that stood in the Cocktail Lounge at Highbury. When the Club moved to Emirates, Fred was moved to Highbury House, the new office building for Arsenal employees and members on matchdays.

GUADELOUPE'S GOOD FOR GUNNERS

Guadeloupe is a small Caribbean island with a population of just 450,000. However, it has helped produce three players who have starred for the Gunners during Arsène Wenger's reign. Thierry Henry, Sylvain Wiltord and William Gallas all have Guadeloupian roots with some of their parents coming from the island.

HEALING HANDS

Former Arsenal manager, Tom Whittaker, was an expert on sports medicine. Having studied anatomy, Whittaker was a pioneer in the use of massage and electrical stimuli in the treatment of muscular injury. When he was the trainer at the Club, he was one of the most famous and respected physiotherapists around. He didn't just treat footballers, he was also visited by the country's leading fighter pilots Tommy Rose and CWA Scott.

During the Second World War, Whittaker was visited by an Indian maharajah who had been unable to use his right arm for the previous two years. Whittaker treated the Indian for a few hours and soon the arm was healed. The maharajah was understandably delighted and offered Whittaker a king's ransom as payment. Whittaker respectfully declined this offer. A few months later, however, he received a selection of Indian silks as a gesture of thanks.

SPONSORED TALK

When Arsenal faced Hamburg in the 2006/07 UEFA Champions League campaign, both sides were sponsored by Emirates. UEFA regulations state that no two teams can wear the same sponsor's name in the same match. Therefore, in each of the two ties, the visiting team changed the name on their shirts to Dubai.

ISLINGTON UNCOVERED (5)

A tributary of the Hackney brook runs under The Arsenal Tavern pub. It drains off the eastern slopes of Highbury Hill and into the River Lea.

HOW BIZARRE! (1)

In 2006, Arsenal's first seven Premiership matches at Emirates netted only two different results: four 1–1 draws and three 3–0 victories. Every time the Gunners took the lead, the match ended 3–0 and every time the visitors took the lead, the match ended 1–1.

19 August 2006 . . . . **Arsenal 1–1 Aston Villa**
9 September 2006 . . . . **Arsenal 1–1 Middlesbrough**
23 September 2006 . . . . **Arsenal 3–0 Sheffield United**
14 October 2006 . . . . **Arsenal 3–0 Watford**
28 October 2006 . . . . **Arsenal 1–1 Everton**
12 November 2006 . . . . **Arsenal 3–0 Liverpool**
18 November 2006 . . . . **Arsenal 1–1 Newcastle United**

HIGHBURY REMEMBERED (2)

The East Stand was 24 metres (80 feet) high and 96 metres (315 feet) long. It cost the Club £130,000 to build in 1936, which, at the time, was a record for any football stand.

PRESENT AND CORRECT

Some Arsenal attendances, great and small:

Woolwich Arsenal 12–0 Loughborough Town	**900**	12 Mar 1900
Arsenal 2–1 Leicester Fosse, Highbury	**20,000**	6 Sept 1913
Arsenal 2–0 Aston Villa, Highbury	**71,446**	24 Feb 1926
Arsenal 3–1 Manchester City, Highbury	**17,624**	26 Dec 1930
Arsenal 3–0 Stoke City, Highbury	**61,579**	20 Sept 1947
Arsenal 4–0 Tottenham Hotspur, Highbury	**69,051**	7 Feb 1953
Arsenal 0–3 Leeds United, Highbury	**4,554**	5 May 1966
Arsenal 0–1 RC Lens, Wembley	**73,707**	25 Nov 1998
Arsenal 1–1 Aston Villa, Emirates	**60,023**	19 Aug 2006

DID YOU KNOW?

As an Everton-mad youngster, Wayne Rooney's hero was Anders Limpar who moved to Goodison Park from Highbury. 'I'd say Anders was my idol,' said Rooney. 'I liked him because he used to shoot and dribble more than Duncan Ferguson.'

THE FAME GAME

The National Football Museum's Hall of Fame, in Preston, features Arsenal legends Tony Adams, Viv Anderson, Alan Ball, Liam Brady, Herbert Chapman, Pat Jennings, Arsène Wenger and Ian Wright.

SEASON TICKETS

The first season tickets at Highbury cost 21 shillings for men, with a special 15-shilling rate for 'ladies or boys'. A Club advertisement boasted: 'This is a very low price, especially having regard to the large number of matches to be played.'

SIR HENRY NORRIS:
A POTTED BIOGRAPHY

His name might not be as familiar as that of Herbert Chapman, David Dein or Arsène Wenger, but Sir Henry Norris is no less significant in the history of the Club. Born in 1865, Norris was a recruitment officer during the First World War and was later knighted in recognition of his wartime efforts. A thin man with a walrus moustache, he made his fortune in the property trade, building many houses in southwest London.

His first foray into football came when he became a director of Fulham Football Club. During his time with the Cottagers, Norris was indirectly responsible for the formation of Chelsea Football Club. Businessman Gus Mears asked him to move Fulham FC to Stamford Bridge and when Norris declined, Mears created Chelsea FC to occupy the stadium instead.

In 1910, Norris became Chairman of Woolwich Arsenal and overlooked the move of the Club to Highbury. Norris was still in charge when Arsenal secured promotion to the First Division in 1919, despite finishing fifth in the Second Division. In 1925, Norris appointed Herbert Chapman as the Club manager.

Norris was Mayor of Fulham and became the Conservative MP for Fulham East from 1918–1922. He was a Freemason and became the Grand Deacon of the United Grand Lodge of England. He left football in 1929 and died five years later, at the age of 69.

HEIGHT RESTRICTIONS

At just 167 cm (5 ft 6 in), Arsenal striker Paul Dickov was a diminutive but powerful presence in the Arsenal squad between the 1992/93 and 1996/97 seasons. However, had the Scot tried to join the Gunners during the 1920s, he might have found it harder to get a game. When Sir Henry Norris appointed Leslie Knighton manager he told him not to sign any players smaller than 172 cm (5 ft 8 in). Joe Haverty would have had the same problem had he played in the 1920s – the Irishman was only 160 cm (5 ft 3 in) – as would 1970s' Arsenal star, Richie Powling, who stood at just 171 cm (5 ft 7½ in).

WAR BABY (2)

The Boer War broke out in 1899 and created problems for a lot of clubs. For a club with such strong military connections, the inconvenience was huge. There were increased duties at the Woolwich munitions complex and this meant both players and supporters of the Club were kept busy. Attendances dwindled during this time, with only 900 fans seeing the Club's record win, a 12–0 thrashing of Loughborough Town in 1900.

THE FIRST INTERNATIONALS

In April 1895, goalkeeper Harry Storer was selected to play for a football League eleven against a Scottish League eleven. However, the Club's first fully international player was Caesar Llewellyn Jenkyns, who was picked to represent Wales against Scotland on 21 March 1896. Jimmy Ashcroft was the first Arsenal player to be capped by England. The goalkeeper earned his first cap during the 1905/06 season.

EMIRATES EXCELLENCE (6)

Nearly 2,000 computer drawings were used for the design of the 35 concessions, 18 kitchens, 22 bars and the main support kitchen at Emirates Stadium.

SNOW STOPPING 'EM

It would be fair to say that the fans of Royal Arsenal were enthusiastic in the 1880s. So many fans turned up to home matches that latecomers had trouble seeing the action on the pitch. The Club used wagons – obtained from the neighbouring barracks – for fans to stand on. When, in 1889, the team faced the Swifts in an FA Cup qualifying round, heavy snow had fallen on the pitch. Rather than have the game postponed, many of the 8,000 attending fans simply rolled up their sleeves and cleared the snow themselves.

HIGHBURY'S FIRST AND LAST GOALS

The first Arsenal goal at Highbury was scored by George Jobey on 6 September 1913. The final goal scored at the stadium was netted by Thierry Henry on 7 May 2006.

	George Jobey	**Thierry Henry**
Born:	Newcastle, 1886	Paris, 1977
Other clubs:	Newcastle United, Bradford Park, Hamilton Academical, Leicester City, Northampton Town	Monaco, Juventus, Barcelona

FULL CYCLE

In the 1800s, many fans would ride penny farthing bicycles through London's Blackwall Tunnel to see Royal Arsenal play. Today, some fans still prefer to cycle on matchday and thanks to the extensive bike-parking facilities at Emirates Stadium, this is an easy option. The cycle parking can be found behind Highbury House and opens two hours before kick-off and for one hour after the match.

WHEN ROBIN MET PATRICK

Having signed his first contract with the Club, Robin van Persie first met his new team-mates in April 2004. He was wearing blue and white trousers and captain Patrick Vieira was quick to point out that these were the colours of Arsenal's arch-rivals Tottenham Hotspur.

WHAT'S IN A NAME? (3)

A family history website has revealed how many people around the world are named after animals or famous film characters. In 2006, 36 babies were called Arsenal.

GREAT GOALS (4)

Ian Wright
28 August 1993 • Arsenal 2 Everton 0
Premiership, Highbury

Ian Wright scored 23 League goals during this campaign. For this one, he received the ball on the edge of the area and juggled it from knee to knee, outwitting Matt Jackson in the process. Now all that was needed was the finish – easier said than done in a crowded area from a tight angle. However, Wright made it look so easy as he lobbed Neville Southall and trotted to his adoring fans in the North Bank.

SHARE AND SHARE ALIKE

The Club – then called Woolwich Arsenal – became a limited company in 1893 when it issued 4,000 shares costing £1 each. These were snapped up by manual munitions workers who lived near the ground in Woolwich.

THE 49-MATCH UNBEATEN RUN (2)

Including own goals, 16 players scored 112 goals between them:

Thierry Henry 39
Robert Pires 23
Freddie Ljungberg 10
Jose Antonio Reyes 8
Dennis Bergkamp 7
Gilberto Silva 4
Jermaine Pennant 3
Patrick Vieira 3
Sylvain Wiltord 3
Edu 2
Sol Campbell 1
Francesc Fabregas 1
Nwankwo Kanu 1
Kolo Toure 1
Ashley Cole 1
Own goals 5

TAKING CARE

When George Graham left the Club in February 1995, his assistant manager Stewart Houston was appointed caretaker manager. Houston guided the Club to a European Cup Winners' Cup Final. Then, Bruce Rioch became manager and Houston returned to the assistant manager role. When Rioch left the Club in the summer of 1996, Houston became caretaker manager once more. After a month in that role, he left the Club to become manager at Queen's Park Rangers, where he appointed Rioch as *his* assistant manager. Some time later, Houston left Queen's Park Rangers to move to White Hart Lane, where he became the assistant manager to the new manager, George Graham.

GREASE LIGHTNING

Grease on Dan Lewis's jersey was blamed for Arsenal's 1–0 defeat in the 1927 FA Cup Final against Cardiff. A weak shot slipped from the goalkeeper's grasp and he could only help it over the line with his elbow. After the game, Tom Whittaker insisted that the keeper should always wear an unwashed (and hence ungreasy) shirt.

MIND OVER MATTER

Prolific striker Jimmy Brain's name remains secure in Arsenal's history books over 70 years after leaving the Club. Courted by Tottenham Hotspur, Brain plumped for the Gunners and netted 139 goals in the red and white between 1924 and 1931. Brain's feat was equalled by Ted Drake but only bettered by four other players in the Club's history, Radford (149), Bastin (178), Wright (185) and Henry (226).

RUSH'S RECORD WRECKED

Ian Rush had an oft-quoted record in the mid-1980s. Whenever the striker scored, his Liverpool side did not lose. That changed in the League Cup Final of 1987 when a brace from Charlie Nicholas saw Arsenal come from behind to beat Kenny Dalglish's side 2–1 at Wembley. The victory sealed Arsenal's first trophy under George Graham.

HIGH SCORERS

For the 2005/06 season, Highbury was the ground where the highest number of Premiership goals were scored.

Ground	Home Team	Matches	Goals	Goals per match
Highbury	Arsenal	19	61	3.21
Riverside Stadium	Middlesbrough	19	58	3.05
Stamford Bridge	Chelsea	19	56	2.95
Boleyn Ground	West Ham Utd	19	55	2.89
Craven Cottage	Fulham	19	52	2.74

THE THINGS THEY SAY

'Your passion for kicking a ball could land you in trouble.'

A Bristol magistrate warns Eddie Hapgood – future captain
of Arsenal and England – of the perils of football

WHAT A GAS!

Before he became a professional footballer, Ted Drake was a fitter for the Southampton Gas Company, earning just 75p per week. Then Southampton saw him playing amateur football for Winchester City. They offered him £3 a week plus £1 as an appearance bonus.

A KISS IS JUST A KISS

'Naturally, as the scorer, Bastin was the hero of the game. At Snow Hill Station a woman kissed him impulsively and called him one of those soft names that women use. And I do not think it was his mother, either. Bastin seemed to take it as a matter of course. Fine life, a footballer's!'

Daily Express, 3 March 1932

BORING, BORING ARSENAL (6)

Arsenal have won a trophy on every day of the week:

- The 1971 League Championship on a **Monday**.

- The 1970 Fairs Cup on a **Tuesday**.

- The 1994 European Cup Winners' Cup and the 2002 Premiership trophy on a **Wednesday**.

- The 1993 FA Cup replay on a **Thursday**.

- The 1989 League Championship on a **Friday**.

- The 1998 FA Cup Final, among others, on a **Saturday**.

- The 1998 Premiership trophy and two League Cups on a **Sunday**.

A PROPER CHARLIE

'For the teenagers, the spirit of the new Arsenal is Charlie George – long-haired, loping, impertinent and often brilliant. In Islington, he is the fourth-form pin-up. They cut his pictures out of magazines to stick on bedroom walls. There are I Love Charlie badges, and it is said he has had more to do with ending the Skinhead cult than any other sociological factor.'

The Sun, 5 May 1971

BILL'S BREAKFAST

During the Second World War, Bill Shankly was based at RAF Henlow. He played as a guest for Arsenal in the war competition and after each game he would sleep in the Highbury dressing rooms. In the morning he would bathe, eat breakfast and report back to his RAF camp. 'I lived like a lord,' he recalls.

JUNIOR JOY

When the Junior Gunners club was launched in 1983, full membership cost £5. Every Arsenal-supporting youngster who signed up received:

- A membership card
- A membership certificate
- A silk scarf
- A sew-on patch
- A pen
- A metal badge
- A colour photograph of their favourite player
- A newsletter four times a year
- Reduced admission to First Division matches
- Free admission to all Football Combination and Youth matches played at Highbury.
- Organized tours of the stadium
- A chance to lead the first team out before a first-team match at Highbury

RETURN OF THE GRID!

In the late 1920s and early 1930s, radio listeners could follow the action in football commentary games with the help of a grid published in the *Radio Times*. The grid represented the football pitch and was divided into eight numbered squares. A radio voice would call out which square the ball was in so that listeners could follow the action of the game at home – many think this is the origin of the phrase 'back to square one'! The first game ever to be reported in this way was an Arsenal match with Sheffield United, on 22 January 1927. Eighty years later, almost to the day (21 January 2007), BBC Radio reprised this commentary style for the clash between Arsenal and Manchester United at Emirates Stadium. John Murray described the action and James Alexander Gordon called out the grid numbers as the ball moved from square to square.

WELCOMING WORDS

'Sirs, you are very welcome to our house. It must appear in other ways than words. Therefore I scant this breathing courtesy.

'It is our pleasure today to welcome you for the first time to our new ground. That pleasure, great though it is, would have been greater had we been able to welcome you to a ground thoroughly equipped and laid out to its full holding capacity.

'Whilst apologizing to all and asking for their forbearance or such inconveniences as they must necessarily experience on this our opening day, we venture to think, when we state we have only been in possession for some 60 working days, that our patrons will admit that we have got as near to completion as humanly possible.'

Arsenal programme, *1913*

'On behalf of all the Directors at Arsenal Football Club I would like to welcome you to Emirates Stadium, the new home of Arsenal Football Club.

'Our move to Emirates Stadium has been all about a collective vision. We managed to deliver the stadium on time and on-budget, a fact of which we are very proud. It's also very important to thank you, the supporters, for all of your support throughout the past seven years.

'So this is it, we're finally here – our new home. From all the Board, once again, thanks for all your patience. Let's hope we can all enjoy being part of this exciting new chapter in the history of this wonderful football club.'

Ken Friar, on behalf of the Arsenal Board of Directors, Arsenal programme, *2006*

BORING, BORING ARSENAL (7)

On 29 October 1983, Ian Rush scored five goals for Liverpool against Luton Town. However, on the same day, Tony Woodcock also knocked in five for Arsenal in the 6–2 defeat of Aston Villa at Villa Park.

UP THE GUNNERS!

To the tune of 'Anchors Aweigh', this song was sung at Highbury in the 1940s and 1950s. At home matches during the 1960s, the Metropolitan Police Band began to play it as the last tune before kick-off.

> *Send Arsenal up the field*
> *For one more goal*
> *No other team can fight*
> *Harder than the boys in red and white*
> *Never let their glory fade*
> *Long may it glow*
> *So let us all give out with*
> *Up the Gunners!*
> *Up the Gunners!*
> *G O A L!*

In 1925, a supporter called Mr Mitchell sent the following song to the Arsenal programme:

> *As you walk along Gillespie Road,*
> *You can hear the nippers shout,*
> *When the 'Reds' without a doubt*
> *Have put their foes to rout*
> *The lads who grace the Highbury field*
> *Will do or die before they yield*
> *And prove themselves a credit to the nation.*

BROUGHT TO BOOK

Over the years, a number of Arsenal players have published their autobiographies. The titles chosen for those books range from the amusing to the hard-hitting to the bizarre:

Derek Tapscott	*Tappy*
Cliff Bastin	*Cliff Bastin Remembers*
Terry Neill	*Revelations of a Football Manager*
Tommy Docherty	*The Doc: My Story – Hallowed be thy Game*
George Eastham	*Determined to Win*
Bob Wilson	*Behind the Network*
Frank McLintock	*True Grit*
George Graham	*The Glory and the Grief*
Charlie George	*My Story*
Alan Ball	*Playing Extra Time*
Pat Jennings	*Pat Jennings: An Autobiography*
Malcolm Macdonald	*Supermac: My Autobiography*
David O'Leary	*David O'Leary: My Story*
Niall Quinn	*Niall Quinn: The Autobiography*
Kenny Sansom	*Going Great Guns*
Tony Adams	*Addicted*
Paul Merson	*Rockbottom & Hero & Villain: A Year in the Life of Paul Merson*
Perry Groves	*We all Live in a Perry Groves World*
David Seaman	*Safe Hands*
Andy Cole	*Andy Cole: The Autobiography*
Ian Wright	*Mr Wright*
Patrick Vieira	*Vieira: My Autobiography*
Ashley Cole	*My Defence*
Robert Pires	*Footballeur: An Autobiography*

PLAYING THE PENALTIES

Arsenal won the 2005 FA Cup after beating Manchester United 5–4 on penalties. This was the first time an FA Cup Final ended with a penalty shoot-out. Here is how it went:

Penalty-taker	Outcome	Scoreline
Ruud van Nistelrooy	Scored	1–0
Lauren	Scored	1–1
Paul Scholes	Saved	1–1
Freddie Ljungberg	Scored	1–2
Cristiano Ronaldo	Scored	2–2
Robin van Persie	Scored	2–3
Wayne Rooney	Scored	3–3
Ashley Cole	Scored	3–4
Roy Keane	Scored	4–4
Patrick Vieira	Scored	4–5

GREAT GOALS (5)

Thierry Henry
9 April 2004 • Arsenal 4 Liverpool 2
Premiership, Highbury

Having been knocked out of the FA Cup and Champions League just days before, when Arsenal found themselves losing 2–1 to Liverpool at half time, it was feared that their Premiership chances might also be dashed. Some fans had yet to return to their seats from the break when Robert Pires calmed nerves with an equalizer and just seconds later Thierry Henry powered past a series of Liverpool defenders before finishing coolly and celebrating passionately. He finished the game with a hat-trick and Arsenal proceeded without further trouble to the Premiership title.

HACK ATTACK

Arsenal players Cliff Bastin, Alex James, Adrian Clarke and Alan Smith all became journalists after hanging up their boots.

GILBERTO SIGNS FOR COLCHESTER!

Readers of the first *Official Arsenal Miscellany* may recall the story of the giant anteater who lived at London Zoo and was named Gilberto. The 120-cm (4-foot) long anteater earned his name when Arsenal supporter Peter Findlay won a competition to sponsor the animal.

Since then, in an exciting transfer move, Gilberto the anteater has moved from London to Colchester Zoo. It is hoped that he will one day father future generations of anteaters.

ALLITERATIVE ARSENAL ACES

Billy Blyth (1914–29)
Brendon Batson (1971–74)
Emmanuel Eboue (2004–)
Francesc Fabregas (2003–)
George Graham (1966–72 and 1986–95)
George Grant (1911–14)
Gilles Grimandi (1997–2002)
John Jensen (1992–96)
Malcolm MacDonald (1976–79)
Sebastian Svard (2002–05)
Stefan Schwarz (1994–95)

MAGIC NUMBERS: 5 OUT OF 5

- Peter Marinello scored five goals in 51 appearances for the Club.
- The lowest ever attendance at Highbury came when 4,554 turned up to watch Arsenal lose 3–0 to Leeds United on 5 May 1966.
- Royal Arsenal's first match after turning professional took place on 5 September 1891. The opponents were Sheffield United.
- On 5 May 1990, David O'Leary passed George Armstrong's record of 500 League appearances for the Club when he turned out in a 2–2 draw at Norwich City. He totalled 722 appearances in all.
- Rami Shaaban made five appearances for Arsenal.

HEAD TO HEAD

Arsenal have had a number of significant matches with Chelsea over the years. Here are some of the most memorable:

- On 22 April 1933, the Gunners won the Premiership title thanks to a 3–1 victory over Chelsea at Stamford Bridge.

- On 24 April 1934 Arsenal won the title again at Stamford Bridge, thanks to a 2–2 draw with Chelsea.

- On 2 February 1991, Arsenal lost the only match of their title-winning League campaign, 2–1 to Chelsea at Stamford Bridge. (Manager George Graham maintains that had defender Steve Bould not had to leave the pitch owing to injury, his team would have won the match.)

- On 18 February 1998, the Gunners went out of the League Cup at the semi-final stage after losing 3–1 to Chelsea at Stamford Bridge. Had the Double-winning Gunners won this tie, they might have won a Treble that season.

All four of the above ties took place at Stamford Bridge. However, an Arsenal v Chelsea fixture of greater significance took place at Highbury on 31 January 1925. This was a special match played to experiment with proposed changes to the laws of the game governing the offside rule. As a result of this match the rules were changed the following season, making two and not three defending players necessary for keeping an attacking player onside.

HEADS YOU WIN

When Thierry Henry nodded home the opening goal in Arsenal's 2–0 UEFA Champions League victory over Porto on 26 September 2006, the goal was significant for many reasons:

- It was the first Arsenal goal in the south end of Emirates Stadium.
- It was his 50th European goal.
- It was his second headed goal in seven days.

ONE-GOAL WONDERS

All of these players wore the Arsenal shirt at least 50 times but only managed to find the back of the net once during their time with the Club:

Frank Moss . . . . 159 appearances (1931–36)*
Archie Macaulay . . . . 107 appearances (1947–50)
Bill Dodgin . . . . 207 appearances (1952–60)
Don Howe . . . . 74 appearances (1964–67)
Jeff Blockley . . . . 66 appearances (1972–75)
Terry Mancini . . . . 62 appearances (1974–76)
John Jensen . . . . 137 appearances (1992–96)
Eddie McGoldrick . . . . 56 appearances (1993–96)
Nelson Vivas . . . . 69 appearances (1998–2001)

Frank Moss's solitary goal in 159 appearances is actually more impressive than you might think – he was a goalkeeper!

EUROPE: THE FINAL COUNTDOWN (3)

The 1994 European Cup Winners' Cup

First round
15 September 1993 . . . . **Odense 1 Arsenal 2**
29 September 1993 . . . . **Arsenal 1 Odense 1**

Second round
20 October 1993 . . . . **Arsenal 3 Standard Liege 0**
3 November 1993 . . . . **Standard Liege 0 Arsenal 7**

Quarter-final
2 March 1994 . . . . **Torino 0 Arsenal 0**
15 March 1994 . . . . **Arsenal 1 Torino 0**

Semi-final
29 March 1994 . . . . **Paris St Germain 1 Arsenal 1**
12 April 1994 . . . . **Arsenal 1 Paris St Germain 0**

Final
4 May 1994 . . . . **Arsenal 1 Parma 0**

GUNNERSAURUS: A POTTED BIOGRAPHY

AKA Gunner, Gunnersaurus was born in Highbury's North Bank in August 1993 and made his debut at the opening game of the season – Arsenal v Coventry City. The film *Jurassic Park* was popular at the time and the idea of having a dinosaur for a mascot came from child supporters.

He enjoyed numerous UEFA Champions League appearances at Highbury and Emirates Stadium and also away at RC Lens in France. He travelled with the players to Arsenal's match against Dynamo Kiev and made a special visit to the Children's Centre in Chernigov in Ukraine. Since his 'birth', the Club has enjoyed a golden era of success including a European Cup Winners' Cup victory in 1994, three League Championships and four FA Cup wins.

He has made several television appearances and enjoyed a number of visits to the Millennium Stadium in Cardiff. On several of these events he has met other club mascots and has remained friends with lots of them.

One of his favourite trips away was when he went along to the Natural History Museum with 50 Junior Gunners, where they researched Gunner's ancestors. While they were there, two very special visitors came to meet them – former Arsenal players David Seaman and Glenn Helder!

Another highlight was the filming of adverts for the FA Cup. Gunner attended these with all the other club mascots and he relished the chance of scoring a penalty past Chirpy (Tottenham Hotspur) and Fred the Red (Manchester United). He still talks about that today! Gunner is one of the most respected mascots in football, his friendly nature has not only been welcomed from Arsenal supporters but from fans all over Europe.

HOW BIZARRE! (2)

Arsenal beat Sheffield United 3–0 on 23 September 2006. All three goalscorers that day shared the same birthday – 17 August. William Gallas and Thierry Henry were both born on that day in 1977, while Phil Jagielka, who scored an own goal, was born on that day in 1982.

WENGER'S EUROPEAN RECORD

When Arsenal finished runners-up in the 2006 UEFA Champions League Final, Arsène Wenger earned the distinction of becoming the first manager to finish as runner-up in all three European club competitions. In the 1992 European Cup Winners' Cup, Wenger led AS Monaco to the Final where they were beaten 2–0 by Werder Bremen. Eight years later, Wenger took Arsenal to the 2000 UEFA Cup Final where, following 120 minutes of goalless football, Arsenal lost to Galatasaray in the penalty shoot-out. The hat-trick was completed in the 2006 UEFA Champions League Final where Arsenal lost to Barcelona.

IT'S THE ROAR THAT SCORED!

'Arsenal's Roar, which undoubtedly is a very good second best to the famous Hampden Roar, was probably not a little responsible for our win. It certainly gave a thrill to those of us sitting in the stands and the psychological effect on the players, even though it was unconscious, must have been terrific. We could almost put down in the records of goalscorers for this match, Arsenal 1 Sheffield Wednesday 0. Goalscorer, Arsenal supporters.'

Arsenal programme, *1950*

IN PRAISE OF PELÉ

During a webchat with the official Club website, Arsène Wenger was asked which player from the last 30 years he wished could have played in one of his teams. 'I would say Pelé. He would fit perfectly in our team. I would play him up front – perhaps we could play with a three! It would be interesting to see if he was as good as everyone says he was. Would he adapt to the modern game? There are all sorts of questions. He certainly looked to be an athlete before football became as athletic as it is today.'

EMIRATES EXCELLENCE (7)

Emirates is the UK's first sports venue to feature permanently installed giant Diamond Vision video screens from Mitsubishi Electric. Each weighs more than 5 tonnes and is 72 square metres (775 square feet), compared to the 40 square metres (430 square feet) of the Highbury jumbotrons.

LECTURE FROM A REF

On 28 March 1952, referee FW Chadwick gave members of the Arsenal Supporters Club and of other teams' supporter clubs a lecture at the Club headquarters. Chadwick did his best to explain what it was like to be a referee. One of the fans later admitted: 'It occurred to us afterwards that we had never looked upon this much-maligned official as being a human being at all! It was, therefore, something of a surprise to us to find quite an ordinary, decent-looking, normally dressed and homely spoken individual standing in front of us and chatting to us like a pal. We shall, in future, think twice before the usual shout of "Open your eyes, Ref!"'

SETTLING THE SCORE

Much has been made of the highly competitive relationship between Arsène Wenger and Manchester United manager, Sir Alex Ferguson. However, when Ferguson celebrated his 20-year anniversary as Manchester United manager in November 2006, Wenger was full of praise:

'I have seen half of those 20 years from very close up. When you think that the average life of a manager [in the Championship] is one year and seven days, and yet he has done 20 years, then it is remarkable consistency.

'It is also a remarkable achievement and a unique one in Europe at the top level. No one could say the opposite. To do something like that needs tremendous motivation and stamina, and he has had that.

'With us two, it was about competitiveness. I am competitive and I don't like to be beaten. Yes, we have had some heated times but time settles things and there is a respect there now.'

GREAT GOALS (6)

Nwankwo Kanu
23 October 1999 • Chelsea 2 Arsenal 3
Premiership, Stamford Bridge

Arsenal were trailing 2–0 to Gianluca Vialli's Blues in this autumnal encounter at Stamford Bridge. During the closing 17 minutes of this tie, Kanu single-handedly won the game for Arsenal with a glorious hat-trick. His winning goal came in the final minute. As Kanu received the ball, Ed de Goey rushed out to try and smother the danger but the Nigerian disposed of him with a fine shimmy. He then found himself at the byline with two Chelsea defenders guarding the goal. It seemed impossible that Kanu could score but his mesmeric strike curled past the two defenders and into the top right-hand corner of the net.

ROB'S RECIPES (1)

Baked salmon

This is a popular dish at the training ground. Arsenal chef, Rob Fagg, sometimes bakes it with fennel, which should be finely chopped.

INGREDIENTS

Olive oil
1 small shallot
Parsley
1 tomato
150 g (5 oz) salmon fillet, skinned and boned
1 slice of lemon
Salt and pepper

METHOD

1 Cut a square of tin foil, 12 x 12 cm (5 x 5 in), and lightly brush it with olive oil.
2 Finely chop the shallot and the parsley and place on the foil. Add a couple of slices of tomato.
3 Place the salmon fillet on top of the tomato and season. Place a slice of lemon over the salmon fillet.
4 Wrap the foil into a parcel and place in the oven.
5 Bake for 15 minutes in a preheated oven, at 200°C (400°F), Gas Mark 6.
6 Remove from the oven and allow to settle for a minute or two before tipping onto a plate.
7 Serve with steamed broccoli and carrots.

BOB BETTERS BEST

It was not easy to get the better of the iconic George Best. Legendary Arsenal goalkeeper, Bob Wilson, recalls a time he managed it:

'My best save came against George Best in, I think, the first home game of the 1970/71 "Double" season. He was clean through on his own, and nine times out of ten he would have scored. I dived at his feet and plucked it off his toe. It was a trademark Wilson save, my speciality.'

George Best sent a photograph of this incident to Wilson. He wrote on it: 'To Bob, occasionally you get lucky. All the best, George.'

DID YOU KNOW?

During the 1950s, the staff of the Butlins holiday camp and the Arsenal Supporters Club used to meet in June to contest the Billy Ternent Trophy.

IT WAS ALL YELLOW

During the construction of Highbury in 1913, the surrounding streets took on a strange colour. As the terraces that were to become the famous North Bank and Clock End began to take shape, plenty of mud and rubble was required to help build up the embankments. As word of the Club's needs spread, many supporters brought yellow London clay to the site. On route, much of this clay fell off the carts used to transport it, leaving the area surrounding the stadium stained yellow for some weeks.

MAGAZINE MAGIC

The Official Arsenal Magazine has been responsible for some memorable puns on players' names. Their headlines have included: 'In Lehmann's Terms', 'Absolutely Fabregas', 'Herr for Keeps', 'Eboue and Ivory' and 'Diaby-est Boy in London'. When physiotherapist Gary Lewin was interviewed, the article was given the title 'Lewin some, you lose some'.

THE THINGS THEY SAY

*'Bertie Mee had little legs, his backside was near the
ground and when he was the physiotherapist
we used to call him Daffy Duck.'*

John Barnwell remembers the days before Mee became manager

NO MORE FAMOUS FOUR

On 13 October 2001, Arsenal played their first match for 16 years without
any of the 'famous four' defenders in the line-up (Lee Dixon, Tony Adams,
Steve Bould, Nigel Winterburn), beating Southampton 2–0. These four
had been extraordinary servants for the Club:

Lee Dixon 1988–2002
619 games; 25 goals
Honours: League Championship 1989, 1991, 1998, 2002; FA Cup 1993,
1998, 2002; European Cup Winners' Cup 1994.

Tony Adams 1983–2002
669 games; 48 goals
Honours: League Championship 1989, 1991, 1998, 2002; FA Cup 1993,
1998, 2002; League Cup 1987, 1993; European Cup Winners' Cup 1994.

Steve Bould 1988–99
372 games; 8 goals
Honours: League Championship 1989, 1991, 1998; European Cup
Winners' Cup 1994.

Nigel Winterburn 1987–2000
584 games; 12 goals
Honours: League Championship 1989, 1991, 1998; FA Cup 1993, 1998;
League Cup 1993; European Cup Winners' Cup 1994.

The 13 October defence was Lauren, Sol Campbell, Matthew Upson and
Ashley Cole.

ROB'S RECIPES (2)

Poached chicken with a pepper and sweetcorn sauce

INGREDIENTS

500 ml (1 pt) chicken stock
1 small onion, finely chopped
Juice of half a lemon
4 skinless, boneless chicken breasts
1 red pepper, cut into small cubes
1 green pepper, cut into small cubes
1 small tin sweetcorn, drained
1 tbsp cornflour
Large bunch chopped parsley
2 tbsp fromage frais
Salt and pepper

METHOD

1 Bring the stock to the boil.
2 Add the finely chopped onion, lemon juice and chicken. Cover and simmer for 10 minutes.
3 Remove the chicken and keep warm.
4 Add the finely chopped peppers and sweetcorn and simmer for 5 minutes. Season to taste.
5 Mix the cornflour with a little water and add to the sauce, a little at a time, until it thickens.
6 Return the chicken to the sauce and add the parsley. Simmer gently for 5 minutes.
7 Check the seasoning again, remove from the heat and whisk in the fromage frais.
8 Serve with steamed rice or mashed potatoes and peas.

ISLINGTON UNCOVERED (6)

The Sex Pistols recorded 'Anarchy in the UK' at Matrix Wessex Studios near Highbury Grove. At the same studio, fellow punk rockers The Clash produced their *London Calling* LP.

NUMBER CRUNCHING (3)

19 The number of pounds that Arsenal Football Club had in its bank account when Henry Norris decided to move it to Highbury.

THE 49-MATCH UNBEATEN RUN (3)

A total of 33 players were used during this run:

Thierry Henry . . . . 48 games (4,312 minutes)
Kolo Toure . . . . 47+1 games (4,174 minutes)*
Jens Lehmann . . . . 47 games (4,230 minutes)
Ashley Cole . . . . 41 games (3,652 minutes)
Robert Pires . . . . 40+5 games (3,432 minutes)
Lauren . . . . 39+2 games (3,553 minutes)
Sol Campbell . . . . 38 games (3,420 minutes)
Gilberto . . . . 36+3 games (3,131 minutes)
Freddie Ljungberg . . . . 35+4 games (2,851 minutes)
Patrick Vieira . . . . 34 games (2,966 minutes)
Dennis Bergkamp . . . . 29+10 games (2,523 minutes)
Ray Parlour . . . . 18+9 games (1,647 minutes)
Pascal Cygan . . . . 15+8 games (1,437 minutes)
Edu . . . . 14+19 games (1,604 minutes)
Jose Antonio Reyes . . . . 14+8 games (1,331 minutes)
Gael Clichy . . . . 8+8 games (786 minutes)
Sylvain Wiltord . . . . 8+4 games (648 minutes)
Francesc Fabregas . . . . 6+2 games (528 minutes)
Nwankwo Kanu . . . . 4+8 games (531 minutes)
Jeremie Aliadiere . . . . 3+7 games (260 minutes)
Martin Keown . . . . 3+7 games (338 minutes)
Jermaine Pennant . . . . 2+5 games (301 minutes)
Oleg Luzhny . . . . 2 games (165 minutes)
Igors Stepanovs . . . . 2 games (180 minutes)
Justin Hoyte . . . . 1+2 games (91 minutes)
Giovanni van Bronckhorst . . . . 1+1 games (134 minutes)
David Bentley . . . . 1 game (61 minutes)
Ryan Garry . . . . 1 game (90 minutes)
David Seaman . . . . 1 game (90 minutes)
Stuart Taylor . . . . 1 game (90 minutes)
Mathieu Flamini . . . . +5 games (59 minutes)
Robin van Persie . . . . +3 games (16 minutes)
Stathis Tavlaridis . . . . +1 game (15 minutes)

Home	Pld25	W20	D5	L0	F63	A21	Pts 65
Away	Pld24	W16	D8	L0	F49	A14	Pts 56
Overall	Pld49	W36	D13	L0	F112	A35	Pts 121

'+ 1' denotes one substitute appearance.

The main pitch floodlights consist of 196 2,000-watt bulbs. There are 12,000 additional light fittings around the stadium.

──────────────── **ON SONG** ────────────────

In 1971, ITV ran a competition for viewers to write a new song for Arsenal Football Club. In the end, Jimmy Hill won the competition with 'Good Old Arsenal'. However, some of the unsuccessful entries survive in the Club's coffers to this day, including this one:

> *McClintock, Wilson and Storey,*
> *Armstrong, Kennedy,*
> *Sammels, Graham and Mee,*
> *Simpson, Rice and Radford,*
> *Arsenal of our dream,*
> *Mee who made thee mighty,*
> *What a wonderful team,*
> *Mee who made thee mighty,*
> *What a wonderful dream.*

This entry came from Mr LVS Rowe of Gillingham in Kent, who said:

> *'What's to stop you printing this in your programme? There's no copyright. I give you that with all my heart. I'm not even asking for a Cup Final ticket. Being partially disabled I'd much rather see them win on TV. My best wishes to you and everyone associated with the success of the Gunners.'*

PS: In 2005, Jimmy Hill told an interviewer that he had recently received a royalty cheque 'for about £57.20' for the song.

──────────── **THE THINGS THEY SAY** ────────────

> *'I've heard it said that you can't be a football manager and tell the truth. Well, I'm going to have a go at it.'*

Liam Brady when he took over at Celtic, *1991*

BORING, BORING ARSENAL (8)

When Arsenal beat Tottenham Hotspur 5–4 at White Hart Lane on 13 November 2004, nine different players got on the scoresheet. This was the first time this had happened in a Premiership match. Arsenal's scorers were Thierry Henry, Lauren, Patrick Vieira, Freddie Ljungberg and Robert Pires. For the home side Noureddine Naybet, Jermaine Defoe, Ledley King and Freddie Kanoute got on the scoresheet. This was one of five times that the Gunners scored five or more goals that season. The other occasions were: Arsenal 5 Middlesbrough 3 on 22 August; Arsenal 5 Rosenborg 1 on 7 December; Arsenal 5 Crystal Palace 1 on 14 February; and Arsenal 7 Everton 0 on 11 May.

TERRIFIC THIERRY (3)

The last six hat-tricks at Highbury were all notched up by Thierry Henry:

7 May 2006 . . . . **Arsenal 4 Wigan Athletic 2**
14 January 2006 . . . . **Arsenal 7 Middlesbrough 0**
2 April 2005 . . . . **Arsenal 4 Norwich City 1**
5 March 2005 . . . . **Arsenal 3 Portsmouth 0**
16 April 2004 . . . . **Arsenal 5 Leeds United 0**
9 April 2004 . . . . **Arsenal 4 Liverpool 2**

THE THINGS THEY SAY

'I knew my players were ready. After a few years, you just know. It's like working for the weather forecast; you have a feeling whether it will rain or not.'

Arsène Wenger, following the team's 1–0 victory
over Chelsea, *January 1999*

SHORT AND SWEET (2)

Andy Cole's Arsenal playing career consisted of just six minutes, as a substitute in the League match against Sheffield United on 29 December 1990. Arsenal won the match 4–1.

ARSENAL STARS

Ever wondered which Arsenal players have shared your star sign?

Aquarius *20 January–19 February*
Jimmy Bloomfield, Liam Brady, Brian Marwood,
Kevin Campbell, Philippe Senderos

Pisces *20 February–20 March*
Pat Rice, Lee Dixon, Paul Merson, Ray Parlour,
Nicolas Anelka, Kolo Toure, Mathieu Flamini

Aries *21 March–20 April*
David Herd, Martin Hayes, Stefan Schwarz,
Marc Overmars, Freddie Ljungberg, Jeremie Aliadiere

Taurus *21 April–21 May*
Terry Neil, Alan Ball, David O'Leary, David Rocastle,
Dennis Bergkamp, Edu, Cesc Fabregas, Gary Lewin

Gemini *22 May–22 June*
Pat Jennings, Andy Linighan, David Platt

Cancer *23 June–23 July*
Danny Clapton, Jon Sammels, Bob McNab, Patrick Vieira

Leo *24 July–23 August*
Ray Kennedy, George Armstrong, Martin Keown, Nwankwo Kanu,
Thierry Henry, Gael Clichy, Robin van Persie

Virgo *24 August–23 September*
Peter Storey, Viv Anderson, Michael Thomas,
David Seaman, Emmanuel Petit, Sol Campbell

Libra *24 September–23 October*
Don Howe, Charlie George, Kenny Sansom, Tony Adams, Arsène Wenger

Scorpio *24 October–22 November*
Jack Kelsey, Vic Groves, Bob Wilson, Alan Smith,
Ian Wright, Robert Pires, Jens Lehmann

Sagittarius *23 November–22 December*
George Graham, Paul Davis, John Lukic,
Nigel Winterburn, Ashley Cole, Boro Primorac

Capricorn *23 December–19 January*
Frank McLintock, Peter Simpson, Malcolm McDonald, Lauren

THE THINGS THEY SAY

*'It got absolutely stupid last year. Every paper, every radio
station, every TV station, was saying: "George needs to buy a
midfield player." In fact, I actually had a T-shirt made up
which said "I am trying to buy a midfield player!" I was
thinking of wearing it after a press conference after a game, but
eventually thought better of it.'*

George Graham, 1994

MAGIC NUMBERS: 4 OUT OF 4

- Arsenal scored four goals against Manchester United during the
1997/98 League Championship winning season. Nicolas Anelka,
Patrick Vieira and David Platt grabbed one each at Highbury and Marc
Overmars added the fourth at Old Trafford.

- Dennis Bergkamp scored his 100th goal for Arsenal on 4 January 2003.
The goal came in a 2–0 FA Cup third-round victory over Oxford United
at Highbury.

- When Arsenal beat Stockport County 4–0 on 13 April 1914, it was their
biggest victory at Highbury to date.

- Emmanuel Eboue was born in Abidjan, Ivory Coast, on 4 June 1983.

What has become of the 1979 FA Cup winning side?

Pat Jennings won an OBE in 1987. He now works as a goalkeeping coach at Tottenham Hotspur. His son, Pat, is a professional footballer and has played in goal for Irish sides University College Dublin and Derry.

Pat Rice moved to Watford in 1980 and returned to Arsenal four years later as a youth coach. He is now assistant manager with Arsenal.

David O'Leary now works in football management. He has managed Leeds United and Aston Villa.

Willie Young retired from the game in 1984 and since then has owned a pub, run some dog kennels and appeared on television as a pundit.

Sammy Nelson lost his place to Kenny Sansom and joined Brighton and Hove Albion in 1981. He faced Manchester United in a subsequent FA Cup Final, although this time he was on the losing side. He is now a tour guide at Emirates Stadium.

Brian Talbot served as chairman of the Professional Footballers Association and managed West Bromwich Albion among other clubs. He is now manager of Marsaxlokk, a Maltese team.

Liam Brady enjoyed management stints at Celtic and Brighton and Hove Albion, before returning to Arsenal in 1996 to head the successful Youth Development scheme.

David Price moved to Crystal Palace and then Leyton Orient before retiring at the age of 28. He has since worked as a taxi driver.

Graham Rix had a spell playing in the French league, before turning out for Dundee and then joining Chelsea as a player-coach. He has since managed Portsmouth, Oxford United and Hearts.

Alan Sunderland played with Ipswich Town and Irish club Derry City before retiring from the game. He ran a pub in Ipswich for a while before emigrating to Malta.

Frank Stapleton having been part of the team that beat Manchester United in an FA Cup Final, moved to Old Trafford and helped the team win two FA Cups. He has since managed Bradford City, been a specialist coach at Bolton Wanderers and coached in the United States.

Substitute
Steve Walford played for a number of clubs including West Ham United and Lai Sun of Hong Kong. He played for Wycombe Wanderers under manager Martin O'Neill and has since served as O'Neill's assistant manager with four clubs, including Aston Villa.

WINGING IT

Winger Perry Groves was the first player bought for Arsenal by George Graham. He cost £65,000 in 1986. The final player bought for the Gunners by Graham was also a winger – Glenn Helder. He cost £2.3 million in February 1995.

THE THINGS THEY SAY

*'I started clapping myself until I realized that
I was Sunderland's manager.'*

Peter Reid talking about Dennis Bergkamp's
wonder goal against his side, *1997*

YOU CAN TAKE THE MAN OUT OF ARSENAL (1)

George Graham moved from Highbury to Old Trafford in 1972. However, he made his Manchester United debut against his old side, Arsenal, losing the match 3–1.

Season	Div	Pld	W	D	L	F	A	Pts	Position
1893/94	2	28	12	4	12	52	55	28	9th
1894/95	2	30	14	6	10	75	58	34	8th
1895/96	2	30	14	4	12	59	42	32	7th
1896/97	2	30	13	4	13	68	70	30	10th
1897/98	2	30	16	5	9	69	49	37	5th
1898/99	2	34	18	5	11	72	41	41	7th
1899/1900	2	34	16	4	14	61	43	36	8th
1900/01	2	34	15	6	13	39	35	36	7th
1901/02	2	34	18	6	10	50	26	42	4th
1902/03	2	34	20	8	6	66	30	48	3rd
1903/04	2	34	21	7	6	91	22	49	2nd
1904/05	1	34	12	9	13	36	40	33	10th
1905/06	1	38	15	7	6	62	64	37	12th
1906/07	1	38	20	4	14	66	59	44	7th
1907/08	1	38	12	12	14	51	63	36	15th
1908/09	1	38	14	10	14	52	49	38	6th
1909/10	1	38	11	9	18	37	67	31	18th
1910/11	1	38	13	12	13	41	49	38	10th
1911/12	1	38	15	8	15	55	59	38	10th
1912/13	1	38	3	12	23	26	74	18	20th
1913/14	2	38	20	9	9	54	38	49	3rd
1914/15	2	38	19	5	14	69	41	48	5th
1919/20	1	42	15	12	15	56	58	42	10th
1920/21	1	42	15	14	13	59	63	44	9th
1921/22	1	42	15	7	20	47	56	37	17th
1922/23	1	42	16	10	16	61	62	42	11th
1923/24	1	42	12	9	21	40	63	33	19th
1924/25	1	42	14	5	23	46	58	33	20th
1925/26	1	42	22	8	12	87	63	52	2nd
1926/27	1	42	17	9	16	77	86	43	11th
1927/28	1	42	13	15	14	82	86	41	10th
1928/29	1	42	16	13	13	77	72	45	9th
1929/30	1	42	14	11	17	78	66	39	14th
1930/31	1	42	28	10	4	127	59	66	1st
1931/32	1	42	22	10	10	90	48	54	2nd
1932/33	1	42	25	8	9	118	61	58	1st
1933/34	1	42	25	9	8	75	47	59	1st

Season	Div	Pld	W	D	L	F	A	Pts	Position
1934/35	1	42	23	12	7	115	46	58	**1st**
1935/36	1	42	15	15	12	78	48	45	**6th**
1936/37	1	42	18	16	8	80	49	52	**3rd**
1937/38	1	42	21	10	11	77	44	52	**1st**
1938/39	1	42	19	9	14	55	41	47	**5th**
1946/47	1	42	16	9	17	72	70	41	**13th**
1947/48	1	42	23	13	6	81	32	59	**1st**
1948/49	1	42	18	13	11	74	44	49	**5th**
1949/50	1	42	19	11	12	79	55	49	**6th**
1950/51	1	42	19	9	14	73	56	47	**5th**
1951/52	1	42	21	11	10	80	61	53	**3rd**
1952/53	1	42	21	12	9	97	64	54	**1st**
1953/54	1	42	15	13	14	75	73	43	**12th**
1954/55	1	42	17	9	16	69	63	43	**9th**
1955/56	1	42	18	10	14	60	61	46	**5th**
1956/57	1	42	21	8	13	85	69	50	**5th**
1957/58	1	42	16	7	19	73	85	39	**12th**
1958/59	1	42	21	8	13	88	68	50	**3rd**
1959/60	1	42	15	9	18	68	80	39	**13th**
1960/61	1	42	15	11	16	77	85	41	**11th**
1961/62	1	42	16	11	15	71	72	43	**10th**
1962/63	1	42	18	10	14	86	77	46	**7th**
1963/64	1	42	17	11	14	90	82	45	**8th**
1964/65	1	42	17	7	18	69	75	41	**13th**
1965/66	1	42	12	13	17	62	75	37	**14th**
1966/67	1	42	16	14	12	58	47	46	**7th**
1967/68	1	42	17	10	15	60	56	44	**9th**
1968/69	1	42	22	12	8	56	27	56	**4th**
1969/70	1	42	12	18	12	51	49	42	**12th**
1970/71	1	42	29	7	6	71	29	65	**1st**
1971/72	1	42	22	8	12	58	40	52	**5th**
1972/73	1	42	23	11	8	57	43	57	**2nd**
1973/74	1	42	14	14	14	49	51	42	**10th**
1974/75	1	42	13	11	18	47	49	37	**16th**
1975/76	1	42	13	10	19	47	53	36	**17th**
1976/77	1	42	16	11	15	64	59	43	**8th**
1977/78	1	42	21	10	11	60	37	52	**5th**
1978/79	1	42	17	14	11	61	48	48	**7th**
1979/80	1	42	18	16	8	52	36	52	**4th** ▸

Season	Div	Pld	W	D	L	F	A	Pts	Position
1980/81	1	42	19	15	8	61	45	53	3rd
1981/82	1	42	20	11	11	48	37	71	5th
1982/83	1	42	16	10	16	58	56	58	10th
1983/84	1	42	18	9	15	74	60	63	6th
1984/85	1	42	19	9	14	60	47	66	7th
1985/86	1	42	20	9	13	49	47	69	7th
1986/87	1	42	20	10	12	58	35	70	4th
1987/88	1	40	18	12	10	58	39	66	6th
1988/89	1	38	22	10	6	73	36	76	1st
1989/90	1	38	18	8	12	54	38	62	4th
1990/91	1	38	24	13	1	74	18	83*	1st
1991/92	1	42	19	15	8	81	46	72	4th
1992/93	P	42	15	11	16	40	38	56	10th
1993/94	P	42	18	17	7	53	28	73	4th
1994/95	P	42	13	12	17	52	49	51	12th
1995/96	P	38	17	12	9	49	32	63	5th
1996/97	P	38	19	11	8	62	32	68	3rd
1997/98	P	38	23	9	6	68	33	78	1st
1998/99	P	38	22	12	4	59	17	78	2nd
1999/2000	P	38	22	7	9	73	43	73	2nd
2000/01	P	38	20	10	8	68	38	70	2nd
2001/02	P	38	26	9	3	79	36	87	1st
2002/03	P	38	23	9	6	85	42	78	2nd
2003/04	P	38	26	12	0	73	26	90	1st
2004/05	P	38	25	8	5	87	36	83	2nd
2005/06	P	38	20	7	11	68	31	67	4th
2006/07	P	38	19	11	8	63	35	68	4th

*Includes a 2-point deduction for disciplinary reasons.

——— WE LOVE SPURS! ———

On the final day of the 1998/99 season, some very rare words were heard in the home sections of Highbury: 'Come on you Spurs!' If Arsenal beat Aston Villa at Highbury and Manchester United lost to Tottenham Hotspur at Old Trafford, then the Gunners would win the Premiership title for the second successive year. Arsenal beat Aston Villa but despite Tottenham taking the lead at Old Trafford, Manchester United went on to win the game 2–1 and therefore claim the Premiership trophy.

MOVING WORDS

'There had been talk within the Club about moving to a new ground as far back as the early 1970s. Believe it or not, at that time there were serious talks with Tottenham about a ground share, and the two parties had even identified a potential site, at Alexandra Palace. In the end the plan was unworkable.

'By the end of the 1990s it was clear Arsenal had to move, or else get left behind. By the 1998/99 season, a new ground was very much under discussion, and the issue started appearing very regularly on the agenda at board meetings. You can date the serious intention to move from Highbury to that season. The will was there to drive the move through, for the good of the Club.'

Adrian Ford, Commercial Director of Arsenal

'It has been said we went through some difficult times. Had we known all the difficulties we had to overcome, I doubt we would have gone ahead. We knew we had to move. It was a question of whether we would stay in Islington or relocate to a site near the M25. Looking back, we were probably crazy but we know this stadium will put us on a par with the all the strongest clubs who are self-sustaining.'

Danny Fiszman, Senior Director of Arsenal

'The project was vital. It was that or die over the long term at top level. It's as simple as that.'

Arsène Wenger

GEORGE GRAHAM: A POTTED BIOGRAPHY

A strict disciplinarian as a manager, one wonders what George Graham the boss would have made of George Graham the player. Known as 'Stroller' for his easy-going approach to the game, he was nonetheless a skilful and subtle player, and a key member of the 1970/71 Double-winning side. He scored 77 goals in 308 appearances for the Gunners, before departing in 1972. Either side of his Arsenal days, Graham also played for Aston Villa, Chelsea, Manchester United, Portsmouth and Crystal Palace.

When he returned to Highbury 13 years later as manager, Graham quickly imposed an air of discipline on and off the field. His methods paid immediate dividends: he won the League Cup in his first season in 1987. Two League Championships followed soon after, in 1989 and 1991. He then led Arsenal to the first domestic cup Double won by any club, with victories over Sheffield Wednesday in the 1993 finals of the FA Cup and League Cup. Europe then beckoned and Graham landed his final trophy as manager in the shape of the 1994 European Cup Winners' Cup.

He left Arsenal in February 1995 having won six trophies in eight years for the Club. He has since had spells as boss of Leeds United and Tottenham Hotspur. He is currently a television pundit.

GREAT GOALS (7)

Alan Sunderland
12 May 1979 • Arsenal 3 Manchester United 2
FA Cup, Wembley

Thanks to the drama that was condensed into the closing stage of this tie on an incredibly hot day at Wembley, this match has become known as the 'five-minute final' but only one of those minutes concerns us here. United had just drawn level at 2–2, after being 2–0 down, when Liam Brady fed the ball to Graham Rix. Rix sped off down the left flank and crossed the ball. Yorkshireman Alan Sunderland met the cross and pushed the ball past Gary Bailey to win the FA Cup for Arsenal.

First derby

The first clash with Tottenham Hotspur under Wenger was on 24 November 1996, and was his fourth home game in charge. Arsenal won a memorable game 3–1 with goals from Ian Wright, Tony Adams and Dennis Bergkamp. In his first ten years at the helm, Wenger lost just one of 21 north London derbies.

The 21 matches were:

24 November 1996	**Highbury 3–1**
15 February 1997	**White Hart Lane 0–0**
30 August 1997	**Highbury 0–0**
23 December 1997	**White Hart Lane 1–1**
14 November 1998	**Highbury 0–0**
5 May 1999	**White Hart Lane 3–1**
7 November 1999	**White Hart Lane 1–2**
19 March 2000	**Highbury 2–1**
18 December 2000	**White Hart Lane 1–1**
31 March 2001	**Highbury 2–0**
8 April 2001	**Old Trafford 2–1**
17 November 2001	**White Hart Lane 1–1**
6 April 2002	**Highbury 2–1**
16 November 2002	**Highbury 3–0**
15 December 2002	**White Hart Lane 1–1**
8 November 2003	**Highbury 2–1**
25 April 2004	**White Hart Lane 2–2**
13 November 2004	**White Hart Lane 5–4**
25 April 2005	**Highbury 1–0**
29 October 2005	**White Hart Lane 1–1**
22 April 2006	**Highbury 1–1**

THE THINGS THEY SAY

'We gave ourselves an hour for a drive which normally takes 20 minutes. But even then it was a difficult journey. I have never seen scenes like it. Those thronging crowds increased the sense of occasion for us. There was no way we were going to be beaten.'

Bertie Mee recalls the journey to White Hart Lane the evening Arsenal won the 1971 League Championship ...

'It was an amazing night. There were 40,000 locked outside and the coach had difficulty getting into the ground through the mass of heaving bodies. I saw my wife with George (Graham's) wife crushed in the throng and stopped the coach and grabbed them on board. Bertie was bloody disgusted, he was a strict disciplinarian and one of his rules was no women on the bus.'

... and so does Frank McLintock

A ROYAL SUPER-SUB!

Emirates Stadium was officially opened on 26 October 2006 by His Royal Highness, the Duke of Edinburgh.

He took over the role after the Queen injured her back and was unable to attend. 'The strain was sustained at the end of the Balmoral period and has not improved during a busy two weeks,' said a Royal spokesperson. The Duke started at the Arsenal Learning Centre and then received a briefing on the stadium development.

After visiting the Arsenal Museum, he was introduced to Arsène Wenger and the first-team squad at the side of the pitch. The Duke also oversaw a demonstration training session involving children from the Arsenal Soccer Schools and the Junior Gunners.

The event culminated with the unveiling of a plaque to commemorate the official opening of the stadium.

STARTING WITH THE SAINTS

Three of Arsène Wenger's signings have broken their duck against Southampton. Dennis Bergkamp, Marc Overmars and Thierry Henry all scored their first Arsenal goal against the south-coast side. Meanwhile, Ian Wright scored his first League goal against Southampton, his first ever Arsenal goal having come in the previous match, a League Cup tie against Leicester, which resulted in a 1–1 draw.

EUROPE: THE FINAL COUNTDOWN (4)
The 2000 UEFA Cup

Third round
25 November 1999 .... **Arsenal 3 Nantes 0**
9 December 1999 .... **Nantes 3 Arsenal 3**

Fourth round
2 March 2000 .... **Arsenal 5 Deportivo La Coruna 1**
9 March 2000 .... **Deportivo La Coruna 2 Arsenal 1**

Quarter-final
16 March 2000 .... **Arsenal 2 Werder Bremen 0**
23 March 2000 .... **Werder Bremen 2 Arsenal 4**

Semi-final
6 April 2000 .... **Arsenal 1 Lens 0**
20 April 2000 .... **Lens 1 Arsenal 2**

Final
17 May 2000 .... **Arsenal 0 Galatasaray 0**
(Galatasaray won 4–1 on penalties)

HIGHBURY'S FULL-TIME REPORT

League matches

454 players made League appearances for Arsenal at Highbury.
268 players scored for Arsenal in League matches at Highbury. Fifty-one of these scored only once.
922 substitutions were made, involving 152 different players.

FA Cup matches

293 players made appearances for Arsenal in FA Cup matches at Highbury.
110 different players scored for Arsenal in FA Cup matches played at Highbury.
90 substitutions were made, involving 57 different players.

League Cup matches

202 players appeared for Arsenal in League Cup ties played at Highbury.
72 players scored for Arsenal in League Cup ties played at Highbury.
94 substitutions were made in these ties, involving 66 different players.

VIV AND TONE

Viv Anderson and Tony Woodcock were apprentices together at Nottingham Forest and played together again at Arsenal, when Viv arrived at Highbury in 1984. The pair are together still, in a third incarnation, running a sports media business. Viv Anderson says, 'We are still together now in business, although I don't have a hairstyle like his! I keep telling him to get it cut but I think he is trying to recapture his youth so I'll leave him to it! I think it's called the male menopause!'

WENGER INNOVATIONS (4)

The manager's attention to detail is something all those who have played under him at Arsenal have praised. There is no finer example of this than the fact that he arranged for the temperature on the team bus to be turned up to keep players' muscles supple. Wenger was a key figure in developing the Club's new training ground; he even chose the cutlery and chairs in the canteen.*

*See also: Training ground, page 129

JENS'S JOLLY YEAR

In August 2006, Arsenal goalkeeper Jens Lehmann was voted as UEFA Club Goalkeeper of the Year. This reflected a fantastic 12 months for Jens, not just at club level, but on the international stage as well.

- He made two particularly heroic saves during Arsenal's march to the 2006 UEFA Champions League Final. The first came when he denied Real Madrid striker Raul at Highbury. The second was his dramatic penalty save from Riquelme in the closing moments of the semi-final second leg at Villarreal.

- He also made a superb save from Steven Gerrard's penalty when Arsenal faced Liverpool in a Premier League fixture that took place at Anfield in February.

- From the 64th minute of the UEFA Champions League quarter-final with Bayern Munich on 22 March 2005 to the last-minute goal scored by Hamburg on 13 September 2006, Jens kept a clean sheet for 853 minutes (over 14 hours). This is a Champions League record.

- Aside from the third place play-off, Jens played in all of his country's games at the 2006 World Cup Finals in Germany, having secured the number 1 shirt. He saved a penalty each from Roberto Ayala and Esteban Cambiasso in the quarter-final game clash with Argentina, to send Germany through to the semi-final.

- Even Oliver Kahn, his rival for the German number 1 shirt, had kind words for Jens. 'Jens's performance has been flawless,' he said. 'He plays very calmly and balanced.'

- He was named in the World Cup All-star squad.

- Between 1 February 2005 and 12 November 2006, Jens made 61 consecutive starts in the League.

EUROPE: THE FINAL COUNTDOWN (5)

The 2006 UEFA Champions League

First round

14 September 2005	**Arsenal 2 FC Thun 1**
27 September 2005	**Ajax 1 Arsenal 2**
18 October 2005	**Sparta Prague 0 Arsenal 2**
2 November 2005	**Arsenal 3 Sparta Prague 0**
22 November 2005	**FC Thun 0 Arsenal 1**
7 December 2005	**Arsenal 0 Ajax 0**

Second round

21 February 2006	**Real Madrid 0 Arsenal 1**
8 March 2006	**Arsenal 0 Real Madrid 0**

Quarter-final

28 March 2006	**Arsenal 2 Juventus 0**
5 April 2006	**Juventus 0 Arsenal 0**

Semi-final

19 April 2006	**Arsenal 1 Villarreal 0**
25 April 2006	**Villarreal 0 Arsenal 0**

Final

17 May 2006	**Barcelona 2 Arsenal 1**

HAT-TRICKS

The 126 hat-tricks scored at Highbury:

Jimmy Brain	**11**
Thierry Henry	**8**
Jack Lambert	**7**
Doug Lishman	**7**
Ted Drake	**6**
Ian Wright	**6**
David Herd	**5**
David Jack	**5**
Ronnie Rooke	**5**

WILLIAM GALLAS FACTS

- He was the first foreign player bought for Arsenal from an English club by Arsène Wenger.

- He was given the number 10 shirt – normally reserved for strikers – because he felt uncomfortable taking the number 3 shirt. Arsène Wenger also felt that the number 10 shirt should go from Dennis Bergkamp to a defender to avoid subsequent wearers in a striking position being compared to Dennis.

- He once wore the number 13 shirt, because it matched the postcode of his home town, Marseille.

TRAINING GROUND

Prior to 1961, Arsenal players trained at Highbury Stadium and could even be seen jogging around the surrounding streets. The Club then moved its training facilities to the University College of London's Student Union site. In 1999, the Club unveiled a brand new, state-of-the-art training centre a short distance from the village of Shenley. The facilities at the new training centre are the envy of the football world:

- Ten full-size, outdoor pitches, all with under-soil drainage and an automated sprinkler system. Two of the pitches also have under-soil heating. These pitches cover 25 acres.

- There are 45 acres of forestry, in which the Club has planted over 27,000 trees.

- There are six changing rooms, a steamroom, a swimming pool with adjustable floor, a gymnasium, treatment rooms, massage baths, and a restaurant.

- In addition to the playing and coaching staff, also based at the centre are two full-time gardeners, ten groundstaff (including the former head groundsman from Highbury), four catering staff, three building supervisors and the manager's secretary.

Results

Season 2002/03

Arsenal 6–1 Southampton .... Wed 7 May 2003
Sunderland 0–4 Arsenal .... Sun 11 May 2003

Season 2003/04

Arsenal 2–1 Everton .... Sat 16 August 2003
Middlesbrough 0–4 Arsenal .... Sun 24 August 2003
Arsenal 2–0 Aston Villa .... Wed 27 August 2003
Manchester City 1–2 Arsenal .... Sun 31 August 2003
Arsenal 1–1 Portsmouth .... Sat 13 September 2003
Manchester United 0–0 Arsenal ...... Sun 21 September 2003
Arsenal 3–2 Newcastle United .... Fri 26 September 2003
Liverpool 1–2 Arsenal .... Sat 4 October 2003
Arsenal 2–1 Chelsea .... Sat 18 October 2003
Charlton Athletic 1–1 Arsenal .... Sun 26 October 2003
Leeds United 1–4 Arsenal .... Sat 1 November 2003
Arsenal 2–1 Tottenham Hotspur .... Sat 8 November 2003
Birmingham City 0–3 Arsenal .... Sat 22 November 2003
Arsenal 0–0 Fulham .... Sun 30 November 2003
Leicester City 1–1 Arsenal .... Sat 6 December 2003
Arsenal 1–0 Blackburn Rovers .... Sun 14 December 2003
Bolton Wanderers 1–1 Arsenal .... Sat 20 December 2003
Arsenal 3–0 Wolverhampton Wanderers . Fri 26 December 2003
Southampton 0–1 Arsenal .... Mon 29 December 2003
Everton 1–1 Arsenal .... Wed 7 January 2004
Arsenal 4–1 Middlesbrough .... Sat 10 January 2004
Aston Villa 0–2 Arsenal .... Sun 18 January 2004
Arsenal 2–1 Manchester City .... Sun 1 February 2004
Wolverhampton Wanderers 1–3 Arsenal .. Sat 7 February 2004
Arsenal 2–0 Southampton .... Tues 20 February 2004
Chelsea 1–2 Arsenal .... Sat 21 February 2004
Arsenal 2–1 Charlton Athletic .... Sat 28 February 2004
Blackburn Rovers 0–2 Arsenal .... Sat 13 March 2004
Arsenal 2–1 Bolton Wanderers .... Sat 20 March 2004
Arsenal 1–1 Manchester United .... Sun 28 March 2004
Arsenal 4–2 Liverpool .... Fri 9 April 2004
Newcastle United 0–0 Arsenal .... Sun 11 April 2004
Arsenal 5–0 Leeds United .... Fri 16 April 2004
Tottenham Hotspur 2–2 Arsenal .... Sun 25 April 2004

Arsenal 0–0 Birmingham City .... Sat 1 May 2004
Portsmouth 1–1 Arsenal .... Tues 4 May 2004
Fulham 0–1 Arsenal .... Sun 9 May 2004
Arsenal 2–1 Leicester City .... Sat 15 May 2004
Season 2004/05
Everton 1–4 Arsenal .... Sun 15 August 2004
Arsenal 5–3 Middlesbrough .... Sun 22 August 2004
Arsenal 3–0 Blackburn Rovers .... Wed 25 August 2004
Norwich City 1–4 Arsenal .... Sat 28 August 2004
Fulham 0–3 Arsenal .... Sat 11 September 2004
Arsenal 2–2 Bolton Wanderers .... Sat 18 September 2004
Manchester City 0–1 Arsenal .... Sat 25 September 2004
Arsenal 4–0 Charlton Athletic .... Sat 2 October 2004
Arsenal 3–1 Aston Villa .... Sat 16 October 2004

——— EUROPE: THE FINAL COUNTDOWN (6) ———

The 1995 European Cup Winners' Cup

First round
15 September 1994 .... **Omonia Nicosia 1 Arsenal 3**
29 September 1994 .... **Arsenal 3 Omonia Nicosia 0**

Second round
20 October 1994 .... **Brondby 1 Arsenal 2**
3 November 1994 .... **Arsenal 2 Brondby 2**

Quarter-final
2 March 1995 .... **Arsenal 1 Auxerre 1**
16 March 1995 .... **Auxerre 0 Arsenal 1**

Semi-final
6 April 1995 .... **Arsenal 3 Sampdoria 2**
20 April 1995 .... **Sampdoria 3 Arsenal 2**
(Arsenal won 3–2 on penalties)

Final
10 May 1995 .... **Arsenal 1 Real Zaragoza 2**

PAUL PRAISES GILLES

Gilles Grimandi spent six years at Arsenal and in that time he helped the Club win a host of trophies, including the Premiership and FA Cup Doubles in the 1997/98 and 2001/02 seasons. However, for at least one Arsenal fan, Grimandi's finest hour for Arsenal actually came after he left the Club.

The event was Grimandi's return to north London to play in the first match at Emirates Stadium, which was Dennis Bergkamp's testimonial against Ajax. During the match, one of the Ajax players got himself into a dangerous position. Actor, comedian and *The Official Arsenal Magazine* columnist, Paul Kaye, takes up the story:

'The man of the match without a shadow of a doubt was Gilles Grimandi. How wonderful was that challenge on Edgar Davids after he'd rounded David Seaman and seemed certain to score? With one majestic kick on the Spurs player's leg, Gilles put his entire career at Highbury onto a new level.
How disastrous a jinx would it have been for a Tottenham player to score on the opening day of the new Arsenal Stadium? What an appalling thought but thankfully we'll never know courtesy [of Grimandi]. He is now officially a legend in my book with the rare distinction of having achieved that status based on something he did after he left the Club. Top work.'

DID YOU KNOW?

Fulham never won a Premiership match at Highbury in six attempts.

THE THINGS THEY SAY

'By the time I got out of that office, I wasn't only convinced that I was a full blown right back, I knew without doubt that I was the best right back in the country!'

George Male remembers when Herbert Chapman
plucked him from the Arsenal reserves

DINOSAUR DREAM TEAM

Gunnersaurus names his all-time Arsenal eleven:

Goal Bob Wilson
Right back Lee Dixon
Centre back Kolo Toure
Centre back Tony Adams
Left back Kenny Sansom
Right midfield David Rocastle
Central midfield Liam Brady
Central midfield Patrick Vieira
Left midfield Marc Overmars
Centre forward Thierry Henry
Centre forward Ian Wright
Joint coaches Herbert Chapman and Arsène Wenger

THAT'S YOUR LOT!

The last-ever event at Highbury was the 'Final Salute' Auction. It took place on Saturday 29 July 2006. Over 3,000 fans attended and bid on more than 600 items of memorabilia from the stadium. These included:

- George Graham's old desk and chair **(£25,000)**
- The wood-framed hexagonal meeting table from the Managing Director's office **(£23,000)**
- An Arsenal wheelie bin **(£600)**
- The last-ever programme produced for a match at Highbury **(£7,500)**
- The front row of the Arsenal dug out **(£1,600)**
- The Arsenal crest located above the West Stand executive area **(£2,800)**
- The North Bank goalposts and net **(£2,000)**
- The original plans of Emirates Stadium, signed by Ken Friar **(£1,100)**
- A sign from the West Stand locating Blocks U, V, W, X, Y and Z **(£1,500)**

MAGIC NUMBERS: 3 OUT OF 3

- Jermaine Pennant scored three goals for Arsenal – all in the same match against Southampton.

- David Seaman left Arsenal for Manchester City on 3 June 2003.

- Arsenal's biggest win of the 2005/06 UEFA Champions League campaign was a 3–0 victory over Sparta Prague.

THE THINGS THEY SAY

'In 50 years' time … people might still speak about it more than if you win the European Cup.'

Arsène Wenger, *May 2004 (during the latter stages of the 49-match unbeaten run)*

GOING UNDERGROUND

It is well known that Herbert Chapman convinced London Underground to rename Gillespie Road tube station with the name Arsenal on 5 November 1932. On 12 January 2006, Arsenal Football Club had another moment of underground innovation when it unveiled a Final Salute mural at Arsenal tube station. The mural depicts key moments from Arsenal Stadium's 93-year history, and is situated along the passageway to the ticket office at the station.

BRAZIL V ARGENTINA AT EMIRATES

The first international match to be played at Emirates Stadium took place between Brazil and Argentina on Sunday 3 September 2006. Arsenal's new signing Julio Baptista came on as a second-half substitute and his Brazil side won the friendly 3–0 thanks to goals from Elano and Kaka. This was the first time that the South American giants had faced one another on foreign soil. Arsenal midfielder Gilberto also played in the friendly.

DÉJÀ ABOU

When Arsenal signed Abou Diaby in January 2006, comparisons were made between the athletic, combative midfielder and former Gunners' midfielder Patrick Vieira. Arsène Wenger agreed: 'The way he runs, the way he turns the ball forward and tackles, he reminds me of someone I have seen. But he has a long way to go.'

DID YOU KNOW?

Alex Manninger was the first Austrian to play in the Premiership.

ACTION STATIONS

The Red Action supporters group was formed in 2004 to help boost the atmosphere at Arsenal matches. It consists of a cross-section of Gunners' fans and was previously known as The Atmosphere Group, which was founded in 2003. They have created special banners, initiated sing-a-longs at home matches, gone to away matches in fancy dress and undertaken a number of other atmosphere-provoking activities.

THE WORLD AT THEIR FEET

Thierry Henry, Tomas Rosicky and Jens Lehmann were nominated for the 2006 FIFA World Player of the Year award. Henry has a strong record in this award scheme: he finished second in the voting in 2003, and third in 2005. Arsenal Ladies and England striker Kelly Smith was nominated for the women's shortlist. Meanwhile, Freddie Ljungberg won Sweden's Player of the Year award for the second time in 2006. The Swede first won the award – known as the Golden Ball – in 2002.

Tomas Rosicky was named Czech Player of the Year in 2006, which was the third time he has won the award. The other two occasions were 2001 and 2002. Cesc Fabregas and Thierry Henry were both named in the uefa.com Team of 2006.

REIGNING CUPS AND DOGS

In its 'Rapid Response' feature, *The Official Arsenal Magazine* asked a selection of players whether they preferred cats or dogs and whether they preferred tea or coffee. The results make for tough reading for both the dog world and the coffee industry.*

Cats
Ryan Smith
Emmanuel Eboue
Alexander Hleb
Patrick Vieira
Jermaine Pennant
Jose Antonio Reyes
Moritz Volz
Jeremie Aliadiere
Theo Walcott

Dogs
Philippe Senderos
Mathieu Flamini

Coffee

Tea
Ryan Smith
Philippe Senderos
Mathieu Flamini
Alexander Hleb
Patrick Vieira
Jermaine Pennant
Moritz Volz
Emmanuel Eboue
Jeremie Aliadiere
Theo Walcott

* Had he still been at Arsenal when these surveys were done, you can guarantee that Emmanuel Petit would be in the dog camp. He not only loves dogs but once said he would like to be a dog. He has also campaigned against dog-eating in Korea.

A DATE TO REMEMBER (2)

11 September 2001 On the day that terrorists attacked the United States of America, Arsenal lost 1–0 to Mallorca in a UEFA Champions League tie.

FASHIONABLE GUNNERS (2)

'The beautiful blue suits from Austin Reed.'

Bertie Mee's policy for what players must wear

'Thierry embodies a unique sense of modern style.'

Tommy Hilfiger

'I like to mix different styles, a really nice shirt or jacket with some vintage jeans that are a bit beaten up. For me, that's fashion — when you can mix different stuff that you maybe don't think fits together.'

Freddie Ljungberg on the launch of his contract with Calvin Klein

THE THINGS THEY SAY

'Steve and Nigel are like two good bottles of French red wine. The older they get, the better they are.'

Arsène Wenger on Steve Bould and
Nigel Winterburn, *February 1998*

MAGIC NUMBERS: 2 OUT OF 2

- Three years after the number 2 shirt was rested following Lee Dixon's retirement, it was given to Abou Diaby.

- Steve Bould scored two goals in one game, against Sampdoria in the European Cup Winners' Cup semi-final first leg, April 1995.

GENEROUS GERRARD

When Arsenal beat Liverpool 2–1 on 12 March 2006, Thierry Henry benefited from a mistake made by Steven Gerrard. The Liverpool skipper attempted a backpass to his goalkeeper but Henry seized the pass and scored the winning goal.

This was not the first time that Henry had capitalized on a weak Gerrard backpass. When England and France squared up during the European Championships in 2004, Henry intercepted the pass and was hauled to the ground by England keeper David James. The resulting penalty was scored by Zinedine Zidane to win the tie for the French.

THE 49-MATCH UNBEATEN RUN (5)

This was the final match of Arsenal's historic 49-match unbeaten run:

**16 October 2004 • Arsenal Stadium, Highbury • Attendance: 38,137
Arsenal 3 Aston Villa 1 (Goals: Pires 2, Henry 1)
Formation: 4-4-2**

LEHMANN

LAUREN   CAMPBELL   TOURE   COLE

PIRES   VIEIRA   FABREGAS   REYES

BERGKAMP   HENRY

**Subs used: 16 Flamini (for Vieira), 21 Pennant (for Reyes),
11 van Persie (for Pires)**

HIGHBURY REMEMBERED (3)

Between the 1930s and 1990s, there were two box-sized commentary rooms in use at the back of Highbury's East Stand Lower Tier. Situated either side of the halfway line, one was used by the PA announcer and one was used to relay commentary to London's hospitals. Commentary for hospitals was stopped in the mid-1980s and, in 1994, a new booth for the PA announcer was built between the Clock End and East Stand.

DAVID ROCASTLE

'I know David Rocastle. I saw the Arsenal team play with him in it. He was the kind of player I like – tricky and creative. He would find a place with me. You always respond to the qualities the players show you. We would be very happy to have him now at 20 years of age.'

Arsène Wenger, *April 2006*

DID YOU KNOW?

When Arsenal appeared in the 2005 FA Cup semi-final against Blackburn Rovers, beating them 3–0, it was the Club's 25th FA Cup semi-final appearance. This is a record shared with Manchester United.

MAGIC NUMBERS: 1 OUT OF 1

Arsenal lost just one game during the 1990/91 League Championship winning season. It came against Chelsea at Stamford Bridge. George Graham maintains that had an injury not taken him out of the game, Arsenal would not have lost that one either!

THE FIRST COMPETITIVE MATCH AT EMIRATES STADIUM

19 August 2006 • Emirates Stadium • Attendance: 60,023
Arsenal 1 Aston Villa 1 (Goal: Gilberto)
Formation: 4-4-2

LEHMANN

EBOUE   TOURE   DJOUROU   HOYTE

HLEB   FABREGAS   SILVA   LJUNGBERG

ADEBAYOR   HENRY

**Subs used: 11 van Persie (for Adebayor), 32 Walcott (for Ljungberg),
16 Flamini (for Hoyte)**

EMIRATES EXCELLENCE (9)

The exact capacity of Emirates Stadium is 60,432. This is divided in the following way: Lower Tier 24,425; Upper Tier, 26,646; Club Level 7,139; and Box Level 2,222.

HIGHBURY REMEMBERED (4)

Above the ladies' toilets in the East Stand was the Flag Room, where the numerous flags used by the Club on matchdays were stored. They were washed, ironed and dried regularly in the Club's laundry. The room was only accessible by climbing a steep ladder.

EMIRATES EXCELLENCE (10)

There are two Club shops at Emirates. The flagship store, The Armoury, is located at the base of the North Bridge building at the northeast of the stadium. It measures 10,000 square metres (12,000 square yards). A smaller store called All Arsenal is at the base of the North Bridge.

ISLINGTON UNCOVERED (7)

The tower blocks next to Citizen Road, adjacent to Emirates Stadium, were built in the late 1960s. They form the Harvest Estate and are the only high-rise housing to be found in north Islington. They are named after a 17th-century brewer.

2006 UEFA CHAMPIONS LEAGUE FINAL

17 May 2006 • Stade de France • Attendance 79,500
Arsenal 1 Barcelona 2 (Goal: Campbell)
Formation: 4-5-1

LEHMANN

EBOUE   CAMPBELL   TOURE   COLE

HLEB   SILVA   FABREGAS   PIRES   LJUNGBERG

HENRY

Subs used: 24 Almunia (for Pires), 16 Flamini (for Fabregas),
9 Reyes (for Hleb)

ARSENAL AD 2000

In February 1968, Arsenal secretary Bob Wall celebrated 40 years with the Club. He had started working at the Club as a 16-year-old as personal assistant to manager Herbert Chapman. On his 40th anniversary as an Arsenal employee, he gave his vision of how Highbury would look in the year 2000:

Retractable roof 'There will be a cover all round over the spectators and a retractable roof that will be pulled back in good weather to allow healthy growth of grass. We must bring supporters more into our orbit, by providing rooms for meetings, recreation, dances and restaurants.'

Increased capacity 'More seating is required and I visualize a capacity of 75,000 with 45,000 seated. The standing spectators would be in enclosures round the ground in front of the stands so that if there is any trouble the police would have easy access. People don't fight if they are sitting down.'

The heat is on 'Heating of the stadium is much nearer than you think. We would drop an infra-red curtain along the front of the stand to retain all the heat behind it and have auxiliary heaters as you go back.'

CHARITABLE TESTIMONIALS

Former Arsenal striker, Niall Quinn, was the first professional footballer to donate all the proceeds from his testimonial match to charity. He gave the profits from his Sunderland testimonial (more than £1 million) to a range of causes including City Hospitals Sunderland, Our Lady's Hospital for Sick Children, Dublin, and GOAL, a humanitarian organization, one of whose projects was in Calcutta, India.

Since then, a number of other players have followed Quinn's lead including Tony Adams. Dennis Bergkamp donated the proceeds from his testimonial match to four charities. They are: Make-a-Wish-Foundation, Kika, Willow Foundation and The Cruyff Foundation.

IT MUST BE LOVE

'It didn't take a few weeks, a few months or a few years to fall in love with the place, it happened straight away, it really did.'

It was love at first sight between Dennis Bergkamp and Arsenal, *August 2006*

'I love the lads!'

Slogan on a T-shirt Ian Wright wore underneath his Arsenal shirt and revealed after scoring a goal, *September 1996*

'If you identify with Arsenal, it is a moral impossibility not to love Wright.'

Simon Barnes, in *The Spectator*, *September 1997*

'I still love the Club. They were first class, I remember people like Ken Friar, who was always a true gent, good as gold.'

Willie Young looks back longingly, *May 2005*

'I took over at Arsenal because I love to work on the field. I am not at an age where I would like to work in administration.'

Arsène Wenger explains why he chose to manage Arsenal rather than England, *September 2006*

WHAT'S IN A NAME? (4)

The convention whereby the PA announcer only announces the Christian name of the Arsenal team's players, with the fans then shouting out the surname in unison, was influenced by fans of German teams. It was first tried by Arsenal fans prior to kick-off in the League Cup fourth-round tie against Reading on 29 November 2005.

Arsenal fans were asked to vote for their favourite moments of the Club's tenure at Highbury. The top 50 were as follows:

1 . . . . First competitive match at Highbury
2 . . . . Last game in red-and-white kit
3 . . . . Allison's side attract record crowd
4 . . . . Cooper and Ali's world title fight
5 . . . Wright breaks Bastin's goalscoring record
6 . . . . Final game in front of the old North Bank
7 . . . . Arsenal's first game under floodlights
8 . . . . Seven Gunners in the England team
9 . . . . . . The renaming of Gillespie Road station
10 . . . . Arsenal win the Fairs Cup in 1970
11 . . . . . . Final bow for United's Munich victims
12 . . . . . . Arsène Wenger's first Highbury game
13 . . . . Bergkamp fires Gunners into Europe
14 . . . . . Stadium hosts two broadcasting firsts
15 . . . Highs and lows in European competition
16 . . . . Netbusting Gunners go goal crazy
17 . . . . . . Arsène Wenger offers FA Cup rematch
18 . . . . The bust of Herbert Chapman
19 . . . . . . Wenger's men break unbeaten record
20 . . . . Spurs beaten on their first visit
21 . . . . Quinn spoils North Bank party
22 . . . . Lowest attendance for Leeds loss
23 . . . . Bergkamp breaks his Arsenal duck
24 . . . . . . Fabregas becomes youngest Gunner
25 . . . . Three Cup Winners' Cup semi-finals
26 . . . . O'Leary breaks appearances record
27 . . . . Gunners wear numbered shirts
28 . . . . Herbert Chapman's first game in charge
29 . . . . Highbury transformed in wartime
30 . . . . Adams stunner wraps up title
31 . . . . Rutherford becomes oldest Gunner
32 . . . . Graham returns to manage Arsenal
33 . . . . . Arsenal's final game outside top flight
34 . . . . . . Graham's Gunners clinch League title
35 . . . . . Football takes a back seat at Highbury
36 . . . . .TV pundit Jimmy Hill runs the line

HOT SPOT

Denis Compton was famous for so many reasons – his football, his cricket and his Brylcreem Boy status among them. However, a lesser-known moment in his career was revealed by one of his team-mates. George Swindin takes up the story:

'During special training, Denis Compton, who had been clowning in the dressing room, inadvertently sat on an almost red-hot stove. To this day, Denis bears a faint scar in an unmentionable place.'

WENGER INNOVATIONS (5)

'I lived for two years in Japan and it was the best diet I ever had,' said Arsène Wenger when he arrived at Arsenal. 'Their diet is basically boiled vegetables, fish and rice. No fat, no sugar. You notice when you live there that there are no fat people. I think in England you eat too much sugar and meat and not enough vegetables.' Out went the poached eggs and chips pre-match meals, in came more healthy options. He also introduced the Arsenal players to the creatine supplement.

ARSÈNE WENGER:
THE FIRST TEN YEARS (4)

First European tie
Wenger sat on the bench alongside caretaker manager, Pat Rice, for the second leg of the UEFA Cup first-round match against Borussia Mönchengladbach in 1996. However, his first European tie officially in charge of Arsenal came the following season, against PAOK Salonika in Greece on 16 September 1997. Arsenal lost the tie 1–0.

The team was: Seaman, Dixon, Bould, Adams, Winterburn, Parlour (Platt 70), Vieira, Petit, Overmars (Boa Morte 70), Wright, Anelka (Wreh 80). Subs not used: Garde, Upson, Marshall, Manninger. Referee: M Diaz Vega. Attendance: 33,117.

First sale
Eddie McGoldrick was the first player released from the first-team squad by Arsène Wenger. Following 56 appearances for the Gunners, McGoldrick was sold to Manchester City. He never played under Wenger.

First award
The first Premiership Manager of the Month award won by Wenger came in March 1998. He repeated that feat in April and won the Manager of the Season award in May.

First red card
The first Arsenal player to be dismissed during the Wenger era was defender Steve Bould. He was sent off against Liverpool for a second bookable offence in the fourth round of the League Cup at Anfield on 27 November 1996. Arsenal lost the game 4–2.

HOME FROM HOME

Emirates Stadium is only 500 metres (550 yards) away from Highbury.

GREAT GOALS (8)

Tony Adams
3 May, 1998 • Arsenal 4 Everton 0
Premiership, Highbury

Scored on the day Arsenal won the 1997/98 title, rarely has a goal been more loaded with symbolism and joy. This goal epitomized the Wenger revolution and crowned the professional and personal transformation of Tony Adams. David Platt won the ball on the halfway line and fed Steve Bould. The centre back passed the ball through to Adams, his defensive partner. He took the ball in his stride and stroked it home powerfully to make it 4–0.

PLAY UP POMPEY

The Portsmouth squad for the 2006/07 season contained numerous Arsenal old boys. The team included Andy Cole, Sol Campbell, Lauren and Nwankwo Kanu. The Club's assistant manager was Tony Adams.

DUTCH MAGIC

Arsenal's resident magician Marvin Berglas has a few tricks up his sleeve and a favourite is called 'There's Only One Dennis Bergkamp'. Berglas hopes that the skill and magic involved will reflect the way the Dutchman played on the pitch. He suggests that a number 10 card is used.

> *'Balance the card flat on the tip of your index finger. Place a coin on top, keeping them both balanced. The trick is to remove the card without dropping the coin. It's easy when you know how! Just give the card a sharp flick on its edge and, with practice, the card will spin away leaving the coin remaining balanced on your fingertip.'*

When Arsenal played Newcastle United at St James' Park on 10 December 2005, it was the first time the Club had fielded a team with 11 different nationalities. The team was:

Jens Lehmann .... **Germany**
Lauren .... **Cameroon**
Kolo Toure .... **Ivory Coast**
Sol Campbell .... **England**
Philippe Senderos ...... **Switzerland**
Freddie Ljungberg .... **Sweden**
Cesc Fabregas .... **Spain**
Gilberto .... **Brazil**
Alexander Hleb .... **Belarus**
Robin van Persie .... **Holland**
Thierry Henry .... **France**

Arsenal played Hamburg at their home ground in the UEFA Champions League in September 2006. When Kolo Toure was substituted, and before Julio Baptista and Mathieu Flamini came on during the second half, Arsenal were represented by 11 different nationalities again. This was a first for the UEFA Champions League. The line-up at the relevant point was as follows:

Jens Lehmann .... **Germany**
Emmanuel Eboue .... **Ivory Coast**
Justin Hoyte .... **England**
William Gallas .... **France**
Johan Djourou .... **Switzerland**
Alexander Hleb .... **Belarus**
Cesc Fabregas .... **Spain**
Gilberto .... **Brazil**
Tomas Rosicky ...... **Czech Republic**
Robin van Persie .... **Holland**
Emmanuel Adebayor .... **Togo**

GREAT GOALS (9)

Jack Lambert
26 April 1930 • Arsenal 2 Huddersfield Town 0
FA Cup, Wembley

This goal sealed the victory that gave Arsenal their first major trophy. In the 83rd minute, Alex James sent a long ball down the middle of the Wembley pitch. Jack Lambert was challenged by a defender, but managed to shake him off. He continued his run and scored effectively ending the contest and winning the FA Cup for the Gunners.

WIMPY WOE

John Radford and his team-mates used to have a Wimpy meal at Finsbury Park station every Friday before going to collect their wages. One Friday, as the team was going through something of a goal drought, a fellow called Audrey at the Wimpy Bar offered £50 for any player who managed to get a hat-trick. Radford scored a hat-trick in five minutes against Bolton Wanderers the following week and claimed his £50. 'However, [Arsenal defender] Ian Ure made me put the blinking fifty quid back into the pot,' remembers Radford.

ISLINGTON UNCOVERED (8)

The population of Islington is now greater than 175,000 but, in 1801, the population of the borough was only 10,212. Nowadays, nearly six times that pack into Emirates Stadium to watch Arsenal play.

CHRISTMAS CHEER

Until the late 1950s, top-flight matches would regularly be played on Christmas Day. The final Christmas Day match at Highbury was in 1955, when the Gunners beat Chelsea 1–0 thanks to a goal from Tommy Lawton. Two years later, Arsenal played their last ever Christmas Day game, also against Chelsea, at Stamford Bridge. The match finished 1–1.

Arsenal played 17 semi-final matches at Highbury – 11 in the League Cup and six in European competitions.

17 January 1968 **League Cup semi-final first leg**
Arsenal 3 Huddersfield Town 2

20 November 1968 **League Cup semi-final first leg**
Arsenal 1 Tottenham Hotspur 0

8 April 1970 **European Fairs Cup semi-final first leg**
Arsenal 3 Ajax 0

14 February 1978 **League Cup semi-final second leg**
Arsenal 0 Liverpool 0

9 April 1980 **European Cup Winners' Cup semi-final first leg**
Arsenal 1 Juventus 1

15 February 1983 **League Cup semi-final first leg**
Arsenal 2 Manchester United 4

8 February 1987 **League Cup semi-final first leg**
Arsenal 0 Tottenham Hotspur 1

24 February 1988 **League Cup semi-final second leg**
Arsenal 3 Everton 1

10 March 1993 **League Cup semi-final second leg**
Arsenal 2 Crystal Palace 0

12 April 1994 **European Cup Winners' Cup semi-final second leg**
Arsenal 1 Paris St Germain 0

6 April 1995 **European Cup Winners' Cup semi-final first leg**
Arsenal 3 Sampdoria 2

14 February 1996 **League Cup semi-final first leg**
Arsenal 2 Aston Villa 2

28 January 1998 **League Cup semi-final first leg**
Arsenal 2 Chelsea 1

6 April 2000 **UEFA Cup semi-final first leg**
Arsenal 1 Lens 0

20 January 2004 **League Cup semi-final first leg**
Arsenal 0 Middlesbrough 1

24 January 2006 **League Cup semi-final second leg**
Arsenal 2 Wigan Athletic 1

19 April 2006 **UEFA Champions League semi-final first leg**
Arsenal 1 Villarreal 0

THE (OTHER) ICEMAN

While competing in ITV's *Dancing on Ice*, former England and Arsenal goalkeeper, David Seaman, revealed that he used to play ice hockey as a youngster and had trials with several local sides before deciding on a career in football. He finished fourth in the show.

EMIRATES EXCELLENCE (11)

The new Arsenal Museum at Emirates Stadium opened in October 2006. It includes a Legends Theatre and more than a dozen interactive sections including 'The Invincibles' and 'The Arsenal Spirit'. It also includes exhibits such as Michael Thomas's boots from the League title winning match at Anfield in May 1989, and the customized trophy presented to the Club by the FA Premier League to mark its record-breaking unbeaten 2003/04 season.

NUMBER CRUNCHING (4)

£100.8 million The turnover of Arsenal Holdings plc for the six months to November 2006.

The Club coordinated a host of initiatives to give Highbury the send-off it deserved. Each home game of the final season had a designated theme, as follows:

Sun, 14 Aug 2005 ... **Players Day** .... Arsenal v Newcastle United
Wed, 24 Aug 2005 ... **Goal Celebrations Day** .... Arsenal v Fulham
Wed, 14 Sept 2005 .. **European Night** .... Arsenal v FC Thun
Mon, 19 Sept 2005 .. **Doubles Day** .... Arsenal v Everton
Sun, 2 Oct 2005 .... **Internationals Day** ... Arsenal v Birmingham City
Sat, 22 Oct 2005 .... **Wenger Day** .... Arsenal v Manchester City
Wed, 2 Nov 2005 .... **European Night** .... Arsenal v Sparta Prague
Sat, 5 Nov 2005 ..... **Memorial Day** .... Arsenal v Sunderland
Sat, 26 Nov 2005 ... **49-ers Day** .... Arsenal v Blackburn Rovers
Tues, 29 Nov 2005 .. **League Cup Night** .... Arsenal v Reading
Wed, 7 Dec 2005 .... **Boxers v Jockeys Day** .... Arsenal v Ajax
Sun, 18 Dec 2005 ... **Great Saves Day** .... Arsenal v Chelsea
Wed, 28 Dec 2005 ... **Hat-trick Heroes Day** ..... Arsenal v Portsmouth
Tues, 3 Jan 2006 .... **Back Four Day** ..... Arsenal v Manchester United
Sat, 7 Jan 2006 ..... **FA Cup Day** .... Arsenal v Cardiff City
Sat, 14 Jan 2006 .... **1913 Day** .... Arsenal v Middlesbrough
Tues, 24 Jan 2006 ... **League Cup Night** ...... Arsenal v Wigan Athletic
Wed, 1 Feb 2006 .... **London Derbies Day** .... Arsenal v West Ham Utd
Sat, 11 Feb 2006 .... **Home Grown Players Day** ...... Arsenal v Bolton
                                                                    Wanderers
Wed, 8 Mar 2006 .... **Managers Day** .... Arsenal v Real Madrid
Sun, 12 Mar 2006 ... **Captains Day** .... Arsenal v Liverpool
Sat, 18 Mar 2006 .... **Junior Gunners Day** .. Arsenal v Charlton Athletic
Tues, 28 Mar 2006 .. **Decades Day** .... Arsenal v Juventus
Sat, 1 Apr 2006 ..... **David Rocastle Day** .... Arsenal v Aston Villa
Sat, 15 Apr 2006 .... **Dennis Bergkamp Day** .. Arsenal v West Bromwich
                                                                    Albion
Wed, 19 Apr 2006 ... **Records Day** .... Arsenal v Villarreal
Sat, 22 Apr 2006 .... **Kits Day** .... Arsenal v Tottenham Hotspur
Sun, 7 May 2006 .... **Goals Day** .... Arsenal v Wigan Athletic

Ted Drake alone scored 42 goals during season 1934/35.

DAVID ROCASTLE: A POTTED BIOGRAPHY

David Carlyle Rocastle was born on 2 May 1967 in Lewisham, south London. He left school at 16 and joined Arsenal the same year as an apprentice. After two years starring as a youth team player, he signed professional forms with the Club. Making his debut under Don Howe, it was clear that Rocastle was a special talent from his earliest outings in the first team. He won the supporters' Player of the Year award in 1986 and the following year he won his first major honour as Arsenal beat Liverpool in the League Cup Final. He was an ever-present force in the League in the following two seasons, which included the 1988/89 Championship winning season. He was the Barclays Young Eagle of the Year for that glorious campaign.

Although he managed enough appearances to claim a medal in the 1990/91 Championship winning season, it was the first title-winning campaign that proved to be 'Rocky's' best in an Arsenal shirt. He collected 14 England caps and would have added more had injury not disrupted his progress just as his international career was gathering momentum.

Despite his contribution to the goal frenzies that defined the run-in to the 1991/92 season, Rocastle was sold to Leeds United that summer to the dismay of the Arsenal faithful. He subsequently moved to Manchester City, Chelsea, Norwich City and Hull City. He also had a spell with the Malaysian team Sabah. However, he never regained the spark that powered his Arsenal career with any other club.

In February 2001, Rocastle announced that he was suffering from non-Hodgkin's lymphoma. The following month, the illness took his life at the age of 33. He is survived by his wife, Janet, and three children. Arsenal named one of the Club's indoor training facilities after him and, in 2001, his son led the team onto the pitch for the start of the FA Cup Final.

YOU CAN TAKE THE MAN OUT OF ARSENAL (2)

Adrian Clarke was, for a short while, a member of the Arsenal first team, playing alongside the likes of Dennis Bergkamp during his nine first-team appearances. He then moved to Southend United. After spells with a number of lower League clubs, Clarke moved into journalism working for the company that ran the official website of his old team-mate Dennis Bergkamp. He was joined there by fellow scribe Julia Court, daughter of former Arsenal midfielder David Court.

HOW TO QUALIFY FOR EUROPE

On 7 May 2006, Arsenal and local rivals Tottenham Hotspur were both vying for a fourth-place finish in the Premiership, to guarantee Champions League football the following season. Arsenal faced Wigan Athletic at Highbury, while Tottenham travelled to West Ham. Here is how a dramatic afternoon panned out:

3.00 pm	The two matches kicked off.
3.10 pm	Arsenal went 1–0 up at Highbury, thanks to Robert Pires.
3.11 pm	Carl Fletcher put West Ham United 1–0 ahead at Upton Park.
3.13 pm	Wigan Athletic equalized at Highbury through Paul Scharner.
3.35 pm	David Thompson put Wigan Athletic 2–1 ahead at Highbury.
3.36 pm	Tottenham Hotspur's Jermain Defoe made it 1–1 at Upton Park.
3.38 pm	Thierry Henry made it 2–2 at Highbury.
4.11 pm	Tottenham Hotspur's Paul Robinson saved Teddy Sheringham's penalty kick.
4.17 pm	Thierry Henry gave Arsenal the lead at Highbury when he made it 3–2.
4.37 pm	Thierry Henry gave Arsenal a 4–2 lead from the penalty spot.
4.40 pm	Yossi Benayoun put West Ham United 2–1 in the lead.
4.53 pm	The full-time whistle was blown at both grounds. Arsenal had secured fourth spot.

THAT SQUIRREL

During Arsenal's UEFA Champions League semi-final first leg against Villarreal on 19 April 2006, a rather strange interruption of play occurred. Midway through the first half, a grey squirrel emerged from the West Stand and ran across the pitch. It treated supporters to a special cameo performance as it evaded attempts by players and officials to catch it, before eventually being ushered out of play in front of the North Bank. Arsenal supporters had cheered the squirrel on and, when asked about it during the post-match press conference, Arsène Wenger smiled: 'He was quite fast – and dribbling!'

THE CULTURE CLUB

A selection of examples of Arsenal's appearances in popular culture:

- In the film, *Goal 2*, appropriately named actor Nick Cannon appeared as TJ Harper, an Arsenal player.

- *About a Boy* is the title of a film based on Arsenal fan Nick Hornby's novel of the same name. In one of the scenes, an Arsenal pennant can be seen hanging in the room of one of the characters.

- Arsenal receive a mention in The Pogues song 'Billy's Bones', which appears on the band's second album, *Rum, Sodomy and the Lash*.

GREAT GOALS (10)

Charlie George
8 May 1971 • Arsenal 2 Liverpool 1
FA Cup Final, Wembley

The goal that sealed the Double and launched a thousand impressions of the scorer's celebrations. With the scores level and just nine minutes of extra-time remaining, George swapped passes with John Radford and scored from 20 yards out. The exhausted George then lay down on the Wembley turf and raised his arms in celebration.

THE WONDER OF WALES

The FA Cup Final, League Cup Final and Community Shield moved from Wembley Stadium to the Millennium Stadium in Cardiff in 2001 and remained there until February 2007. During this period, Arsenal played in four FA Cup Finals, an FA Cup semi-final, four Community Shield ties and the final League Cup Final. The ties in full were:

FA Cup Final 2001
Arsenal 1 Liverpool 2

Community Shield 2002
Arsenal 1 Liverpool 0

FA Cup Final 2002
Arsenal 2 Chelsea 0

FA Cup Final 2003
Arsenal 1 Southampton 0

Community Shield 2003
Arsenal 1 Manchester United 1
(United won 4–3 on penalties)

Community Shield 2004
Arsenal 3 Manchester United 1

FA Cup semi-final 2005
Arsenal 3 Blackburn Rovers 0

FA Cup Final 2005
Arsenal 0 Manchester United 0
(Arsenal won 5–4 on penalties)

Community Shield 2005
Arsenal 1 Chelsea 2

League Cup Final 2007
Arsenal 1 Chelsea 2

HIGHBURY HIGHS (2)

Following Arsenal's final match at Highbury on 7 May 2006, there was a 90-minute closing ceremony to see the Stadium off in style.

This is the ceremony in full:

The ceremony opened with the return of a marching band to Highbury.

Constable Alex Morgan, the police tenor from Highbury yesteryear, performed 'O Sole Mio'.

Actor, broadcaster and author Tom Watt and matchday announcer Paul Burrell introduced a parade of 'Arsenal Legends', who were escorted around the perimeter of the pitch by Junior Gunners. This parade included Alf Fields, John Radford, Frank McLintock, Michael Thomas, Malcom Macdonald and Ian Wright.

A period of reflection was followed by a parade of trophies won by the Club during its stay at Highbury, carried by the Junior Gunners.

Then came the Arsenal Ladies to display their Premier League trophy and FA Women's Cup.

Roger Daltrey performed The Who classic 'My Generation' and a specially written song entitled 'Highbury Highs'.

There was a parade of Arsenal crests, followed by a balloon release from Emirates Stadium.

Sir Henry Cooper emerged, to commemorate his famous bout at Highbury against Muhammad Ali in 1966.

There was a lap of honour by the current Arsenal First Team.

Presentations were made to distinguished Club members.

Manager Arsène Wenger led the final countdown of the Highbury clock.

A firework display was followed by a giant 'Sky Banner' hung from a helicopter, circling the local area for approximately one hour.

THE THINGS THEY SAY

'I met this Club ten years ago and maybe I met them just at the right time of my career.'

Arsène Wenger on his tenth anniversary
of his appointment as Arsenal manager.

A DATE TO REMEMBER (3)

30 March 2002 As the Queen Mother passed away in her sleep in Windsor, Arsenal were 15 minutes into a home match against Sunderland. They were 2–0 at that stage and went on to win 3–0.

TERRIFIC THIERRY (4)

In season 2003/04, Henry scored 30 goals in 37 Premiership games, won the Footballer of the Year for the second successive year with 87 per cent of the vote, and finished runner-up to Zinedine Zidane in the 2003 FIFA World Player of the Year poll.

RED AND WHITE AND GOALS ALL OVER

On 11 May 2005, Arsenal beat Everton 7–0 at Highbury. The goals came from Robin van Persie, Robert Pires (2), Patrick Vieira, Edu (penalty), Dennis Bergkamp and Mathieu Flamini. This was the last competitive match played at Highbury in their red-and-white kit.

INTERNATIONAL BRIGHT YOUNG THING

On 30 May 2006, Theo Walcott made history by becoming the youngest ever England player in a full international by appearing in England's friendly against Hungary at Old Trafford, aged 17 years and 75 days. England won the match 3–1.

TAKE NOTICE

'MISSION: whatever it takes'

Notice pinned on the Arsenal team's dressing-room
door at the 2005 FA Cup Final v Manchester United

ROYAL ARSENAL FANS?

It has been speculated that Buckingham Palace has been home to some
Arsenal fans down the years. During a reception at the Palace in February
2007, Her Majesty approached Cesc Fabregas, who takes up the story:

*'It seems the Queen follows football and she told us she was an
Arsenal fan. She appeared to definitely know who I was and
we exchanged a few special words.'*

If the Queen is an Arsenal fan, she would be following in the footsteps
of her mother. The Queen Mother revealed her love of Arsenal to then-
schoolboy John Pollex in 1955. As they discussed Arsenal's Denis
Compton, she told him:

'I'm an Arsenal supporter! Didn't you know?'

Additionally, Prince Harry has been spotted enjoying games at both
Highbury and Emirates Stadium.

UNBROKEN HOME

Arsenal remained unbeaten at home during an entire League season on
five occasions at Highbury.

Season	Pld	W	D	L	F	A	Pts
1970/71	21	18	3	0	41	6	39
1980/81	21	13	8	0	36	17	34
1990/91	19	15	4	0	51	10	49
1998/99	19	14	5	0	34	5	47
2003/04	19	15	4	0	40	14	49

SELECTED BIBLIOGRAPHY

Connolly, Kevin, *The Official Arsenal Factfile*, Hamlyn, London, 2002

Emery, David, *Gunning for Glory*, Simon & Schuster, London, 1994

Edwards, Leigh, *On This Day*, Hamlyn, London, 2006

Fox, Norman, *Farewell to Highbury*, Bluecoat, Liverpool, 2006

Fynn, Alex and Olivia Blair, *The Great Divide*, Andre Deutsch, London, 2000

Glanville, Brian, *Arsenal Stadium History*, Hamlyn, London, 2006

Groves, Perry, *We All Live in a Perry Groves World – My Story*, John Blake Publishing, London, 2006

King, Jeff and Willis, Tony, *George Graham: The Wonder Years*, Virgin, London, 1995

Manson, David, *Quotations from the Public Comments of Arsène Wenger, Manager, Arsenal Football Club*, Virgin, London, 2005

Ollier, Fred, *Arsenal: A Complete Record 1886–1992*, Breedon Books, Derby, 1992

Rees, Jasper, *Wenger: The Making Of A Legend*, Short Books, London, 2003

Rose, Joe, *Arsenal Player by Player*, Hamlyn, London, 2004

Sims, David, *Arsenal Memories and Marble Halls*, Pavilion Books, London, 2000

Soar, Phil and Tyler, Martin, *The Official Illustrated History of Arsenal*, Hamlyn, London, 2004

Spurling, Jon, *Rebels for the Cause – The Alternative History of Arsenal Football Club*, Mainstream Publishing, Edinburgh, 2004

Tossell, David, *Seventy-one Guns: The Year of the First Arsenal Double*, Mainstream Publishing, Edinburgh, 2003

MAIN ONLINE SOURCES

The Official Arsenal Website: http://www.arsenal.com

Arseweb: http://www.arseweb.com

The Guardian Football Knowledge:
http://football.guardian.co.uk/theknowledge/

OTHER SOURCES

Arsenal Football Club Matchday Programmes

The Official Arsenal Magazine

The Official Arsenal Handbook

The Official Arsenal Annual

The Spectator magazine